Practical social wor

Published in conjunction with
the British Association of Social Worker

| B A S W |

Social work is at an important stage in its development. The profession is facing fresh challenges to work flexibly in fast-changing social and organisational environments. New requirements for training are also demanding a more critical and reflective, as well as more highly skilled, approach to practice.

The British Association of Social Workers (**www.basw.co.uk**) has always been conscious of its role in setting guidelines for practice and in seeking to raise professional standards. The concept of the *Practical Social Work* series was conceived to fulfil a genuine professional need for a carefully planned, coherent series of texts that would stimulate and inform debate, thereby contributing to the development of practitioners' skills and professionalism.

Newly relaunched, the series continues to address the needs of all those who are looking to deepen and refresh their understanding and skills. It is designed for students and busy professionals alike. Each book marries practice issues and challenges with the latest theory and research in a compact and applied format. The authors represent a wide variety of experience both as educators and practitioners. Taken together, the books set a standard in their clarity, relevance and rigour.

A list of new and best-selling titles in this series follows overleaf. A comprehensive list of titles available in the series, and further details about individual books, can be found online at: www.palgrave.com/socialworkpolicy/basw

---

Series standing order **ISBN 0–333–80313–2**

You can receive future titles in this series as they are published by placing a standing order. Please contact your bookseller or, in the case of difficulty, contact us at the address below with your name and address, the title of the series and the ISBN quoted above.

Customer Services Department, Macmillan Distribution Ltd, Houndmills, Basingstoke, Hampshire RG21 6XS, England

---

Practical social work series

Editor: Jo Campling

New and best-selling titles

Robert Adams *Empowerment, Participation and Social Work* (4th edition)

Sarah Banks *Ethics and Values in Social Work* (3rd edition)

James G. Barber *Social Work with Addictions* (3rd edition)

Christine Bigby and Patsie Frawley *Social Work Practice and Intellectual Disability*

Suzy Braye and Michael Preston-Shoot *Practising Social Work Law* (3rd edition)

Veronica Coulshed and Joan Orme *Social Work Practice* (4th edition)

Veronica Coulshed and Audrey Mullender with David N. Jones and Neil Thompson *Management in Social work* (3rd edition)

Lena Dominelli *Anti-Racist Social Work* (3rd edition)

Celia Doyle *Working with Abused Children* (3rd edition)

Tony Jeffs and Mark K. Smith (editors) *Youth Work Practice* **new!**

Joyce Lishman *Communication in Social Work* (2nd edition)

Paula Nicolson, Rowan Bayne and Jenny Owen *Applied Psychology for Social Workers* (3rd edition)

Michael Oliver and Bob Sapey *Social Work with Disabled People* (3rd edition)

Joan Orme and David Shemmings *Developing Research Based Social Work Practice* **new!**

Terence O'Sullivan *Decision Making in Social Work* (2nd edition) **new!**

Judith Phillip, Mo Ray and Mary Marshall *Social Work with Older People* (4th edition)

Michael Preston-Shoot *Effective Groupwork* (2nd edition)

Steven Shardlow and Mark Doel *Practice Learning and Teaching*

Jerry Tew *Working with Mental Distress* **new!**

Neil Thompson *Anti-Discriminatory Practice* (4th edition)

Derek Tilbury *Working with Mental Illness* (2nd edition)

Alan Twelvetrees *Community Work* (4th edition)

Jerry Tew

social approaches to mental distress

First published 2011 by
PALGRAVE MACMILLAN

Palgrave Macmillan in the UK is an imprint of Macmillan Publishers Limited, registered in England, company number 785998, of Houndmills, Basingstoke, Hampshire RG21 6XS.

Palgrave Macmillan in the US is a division of St Martin's Press LLC, 175 Fifth Avenue, New York, NY 10010.

Palgrave Macmillan is the global academic imprint of the above companies and has companies and representatives throughout the world.

Palgrave® and Macmillan® are registered trademarks in the United States, the United Kingdom, Europe and other countries

ISBN 978-0-230-54507-6

This book is printed on paper suitable for recycling and made from fully managed and sustained forest sources. Logging, pulping and manufacturing processes are expected to conform to the environmental regulations of the country of origin.

A catalogue record for this book is available from the British Library.

A catalog record for this book is available from the Library of Congress.

10 9 8 7 6 5 4 3 2 1
20 19 18 17 16 15 14 13 12 11

Printed in China

To the 'Moving On' crew and other service-user, survivor, carer and practitioner colleagues who have given me the inspiration to write this book

Contents

Illustrations

Acknowledgements

The author and publisher wish to thank the following publishers, organizations and authors for granting permission to reproduce copyright material: the Department of Health, for Box 1.2, originally from *The Ten Essential Shared Capabilities: A Framework for the Whole of the Mental Health Workforce* (London: Department of Health, 2004), reproduced under Crown Copyright; the Royal College of Psychiatrists for Table 3.1, original data presented in P. Bebbington, D. Bhugra, T. Bhugra, N. Singleton, M. Farrell, R. Jenkins, G. Lewis, and H. Meltzer, 'Psychosis, victimisation and childhood disadvantage: Evidence from the second British National Survey of Psychiatric Morbidity', *British Journal of Psychiatry* 185: 220–6 (London: 2004); Marius Romme and Sandra Escher for the excerpt in Box 7.1 from M.L.'s story, in M. Romme and S. Escher, *Accepting Voices* (London: MIND, 1993); Jo Smith and David Shiers for Table 8.1, originally from 'Catching them young', *Mental Health Today* 10(5): 32–3 (Brighton: Pavilion Publishing, 2010); the Scottish Recovery Network for the excerpt in Box 9.1, from 'There is more to me than my mental health', in *Journeys of Recovery*, www.scottishrecovery.net/Narrative-Research-Project/narrativeresearch-project.html (2006); and the Mental Health Providers Forum and Triangle Consulting for Fig 11.1, the Mental Health Recovery Star taken from MacKeith and Burns, *The Recovery Star: User Guide* (2nd ed.) and *The Recovery Star: Organisation Guide* (2nd ed.) (London: Mental Health Providers Forum, 2010).

Every effort has been made to trace all copyright holders, but if any have been inadvertently overlooked, the publishers will be pleased to make the necessary arrangements at the first opportunity.

Introduction

In recent years, there has been a resurgence of interest in exploring mental distress and recovery within a social context (Cohen, 2000; Repper and Perkins, 2003; Tew, 2005a). This shift has been reflected in policy developments, such the New Horizons strategy in England (Department of Health, 2009), with similar developments taking place elsewhere in the world. Much of the impetus for this change has come from people who use mental health services whose experience of conventional provision has sometimes felt more disabling than enabling – both in how services are delivered and in the ways of thinking about mental distress that underpin them.

Instead of a 'coercive [and] lifelong ... system with medication compliance as its most important tenet', organisations such as the National Empowerment Centre in the USA have argued for a very different approach, based on the idea that 'your distress is due to a combination of losses, traumas and lack of supports', and that 'you can completely recover' (Fisher and Ahern, quoted in Mulligan, 2001, p. 17). This challenges the extent to which people have become 'stuck in a medical interpretation of their experiences' that leaves them feeling 'different to normal people' (Mead and MacNeil, 2004, p. 7).

This shift in perspective, and a focus on what can best enable people to reclaim valued and productive lives, is setting a new agenda for professional practice for all mental health professions. In Britain, this is reflected in the introduction of the Ten Essential Shared Capabilities for all mental health workers, which situates socially oriented capabilities at the core of practice (Department of Health, 2004).

This book sets out the values, theoretical understandings, research base and approaches to practice which underpin a social approach to mental health practice. My focus is on those forms of mental distress, such as depression or psychosis, that are not the

1

result of dementia or other degenerative brain diseases. Although written for social workers in the first instance, the book aims to be of relevance to mental health practitioners of all disciplines.

The components of a social approach

Fundamental to a social approach is the idea of being alongside people as they reclaim a life that is meaningful and satisfying to them – one that involves participating in the mainstream social world and taking on roles that are valued within social, family, employment and other domains. As part of this, people may need help in making sense of what has happened to them – and how their social experiences may have contributed to their mental distress. Effective practice involves engaging with, not just the person experiencing mental distress, but also their family and social networks, employers, faith leaders and others within their wider social world – both to develop wider systems of support or avert potential social exclusion, and to resolve issues that may have emerged within interpersonal relationships.

In order to work in this way, a social approach requires a value base that is oriented towards partnership and emancipation, recognises the expertise of service users and carers, and sees people in relation to their wider social context – and this is explored in Chapter 1. In Chapter 2, we move outside 'illness' models to explore how we may understand mental health and mental distress in ways that are grounded in people's experiences rather than diagnostic categories. This also suggests a new way of understanding the relationship between the social, the biological and the psychological.

Where social approaches have tended to lag behind medical perspectives has been in the development of a coherent body of theory backed up by research evidence. Chapter 3 provides an overview of research findings in relation to how adverse social circumstances and life events may contribute to an increased likelihood of suffering mental distress. Chapter 4 explores the underlying theme of power relations and how these may undermine our capacity for personal agency to the point at which we start to experience mental distress; and, conversely, how accessing social capital and productive forms of power may be supportive of our mental health and our recovery from mental distress.

In Chapter 5 we look in more detail at how we may internalise our social experiences – and how these become reflected in specific adaptations in how we think, feel or relate to others. In turn, these personality adaptations and coping strategies may confer on us particular areas of resilience or vulnerability. It is these that may make the difference as to whether or not a subsequent 'problem of living' may tip us over into an experience of mental distress. In Chapter 6, we explore how, although our interactions with family and wider social systems can be supportive for us, they can also be sources of stress and tension. Relationship difficulties may have a serious impact on our mental health and, conversely, our mental distress may also have a major adverse impact on our personal relationships.

There has been a lack of clear and generally understood *social* models of mental distress by which to guide practice. In Chapter 7, I develop two social models of mental distress. The first explores the build-up of mental distress: how current experiences of stress and humiliation may interact with the legacy of previous adverse social experiences to trigger unease which may lead on into mental distress. However, the story does not end here: a second model explores how the social consequences of mental distress may be at least as damaging as the distress itself – and how one may become trapped within a vicious circle of escalating distress, stigma and social exclusion.

The final chapters of the book focus on practice. Chapter 8 reviews developments in early intervention and crisis resolution: holistic approaches that foreground social issues and social inclusion, and which can be crucial in steering people away from longer-term 'careers' within mental health services. Chapter 9 explores the potential of recovery-oriented practice, looking at how social supports and interventions may be important alongside the more personal aspects of people's recovery journeys. Chapter 10 provides a critique of discourses of 'risk minimisation' and attempts at risk prediction – and explores more collaborative approaches to safeguarding and 'positive risk-taking'. In Chapter 11, we look at how processes of assessment and Action Planning may be inclusive of family and friends, and how they may put people in charge of their recovery, maintaining their wellbeing and managing any crises or setbacks. This may be facilitated by people using personal budgets to organise their support in ways that are most helpful to them.

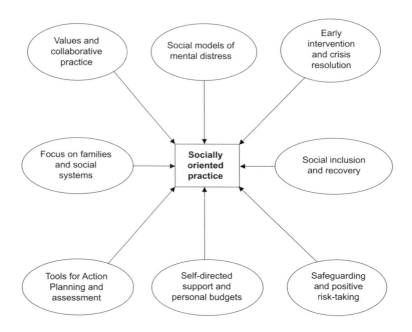

Figure 1 Components of a social approach

Language and terminology

Perhaps more than in any other field of health and social care, language relating to mental health issues is contested and contentious. The ways of seeing and identities that arise out of the use of particular terminologies can have profound effects, not just on the person who may be experiencing distress, but also on their families and friends, and on their relationships with mental health practitioners.

The label 'mental illness', and the diagnostic terminologies that go with a biomedical approach, can impact on how people see themselves and are seen by others: it can situate them as passive 'patients' waiting to be cured by experts, and certain aspects of their experience may become invalidated or marginalized. For this reason, I will avoid the use of 'illness' language except to explore the often unintended implications of certain terms.

Equally contentious can be terms such as 'service user' and 'carer', which construct people's status and identity solely in terms of their relationship to mental health services, or the caring aspect of their relationship with someone who may be vulnerable. Such terms may have political value in terms of building alliances and demanding to be heard by professional systems – and also in claiming particular knowledge and expertise on the basis of particular standpoints. However, they are also limiting: one ceases to be a whole person when one becomes either a service user or a carer, as one is implicitly denied any aspirations for a life beyond the confines of one's ascribed identity. These labels may lock one into one-sided and non-reciprocal relationships: service users can no longer care about others, and carers can no longer expect to be cared about as persons in their own right. Again, I have sought to avoid such terms except where it is this aspect of people's identities that may be most relevant.

So what forms of language can we use without doing violence to people's identities and aspirations? First, I have tried wherever possible to use inclusive terms, such as 'we', 'one' or 'people', which reinforce the idea that we may all experience mental health difficulties at some point in our lives, and we may all take on a role of caring for (or about) someone else who is experiencing mental health difficulties. This book is not about separating the world into divisions of 'us' and 'them'.

Secondly, I have chosen to use the term 'mental distress' to denote experiences that go beyond the upsets, losses and challenges of everyday life. This is a term with which many people who use mental health services are comfortable as it does not imply illness, incapacity or inferiority. My desire not to categorise people by the use of terms such as 'the mentally ill' or 'service users' leads me to fall back on slightly unwieldy phrases such as 'people who are experiencing mental distress' throughout much of the text. I trust that the reader will appreciate the rationale for this.

1 | Values and working relationships

While the application of a social approach to working with mental distress requires the development of models of understanding and strategies for bringing about change, effective practice depends more than anything on developing an appropriate value base and establishing relationships that are affirmative and supportive. This may require some rethinking of more traditional notions of 'professionalism' and any assumption that the practitioner can somehow deliver 'evidence-based practice' without engaging in the complexities of developing a working relationship.

Personal and professional values

Values may be defined as beliefs, attitudes and expectations which can define how we see ourselves and other people, what we see as important, what we aspire to, what we like and dislike, and how we behave and expect others to behave towards us. While our values are personal to us, they may be strongly influenced by the social, cultural and moral contexts in which we are brought up and within which we are currently situated.

Overlaying (and sometimes conflicting with) personal values are the explicit and implicit professional value systems into which practitioners are inducted. These can:

- influence practitioners' basic attitudes and ways of relating to service users, families and carers;
- define a professional identity;
- determine what may be seen as important or unimportant in people's lives;
- inform judgements as to what is 'normal' or 'acceptable';
- construct implicit models of mental distress.

What can become firmly embedded within professional value systems – social as well as medical – are constructions of 'us' and 'them' which place a distance, and a power relationship, between practitioners and service users and carers (and also between different professional disciplines). Fundamental to a social approach is overcoming such distinctions – and seeking to establish relationships of partnership and co-production.

In learning to discuss and reason about values, it is important to recognise that values are not absolutes and may sometimes be in contradiction to one another (for example, where may a duty to protect override a commitment to self-determination?). Thus a professional value base is by no means straightforward or static – practice involves a continual balancing of different values and how they link to a particular situation.

Service users and carers as experts by experience and agents of their own recovery

Over recent years we have seen a major change in how service users and carers are situated within the discourses of mental heath service provision. Instead of service users being seen as passive recipients of plans of treatment and care devised by professional experts, and carers being marginalised as onlookers, those who have lived experience are starting to be recognised as experts on the basis of this experience: they may know, better than anyone else, what may actually be going on, and may also have built up a unique expertise in terms of ways of understanding and developing coping strategies (Beresford, 2003).

This starts to challenge the notion that professionals 'know best' and that their theories and evidence are inherently superior to any insights that those directly involved may have about their situation. It fundamentally changes the terms of the relationship to one in which everyone's voice is valued, and differences in perspective are not seen as 'difficulties to be overcome' but as opportunities to develop a deeper understanding of the situation and possible ways forward. Such an inclusive approach to understanding, which is rooted in an ongoing dialogue with those who have firsthand experience of their situation, is fundamental to a social approach.

People with lived experience of mental distress have been at the heart of the recovery movement which seeks to put people in the 'driving seat' of their own recovery – and situate practitioners as allies or enablers of this process. Their primary role is not to 'treat' or 'care' for people, but to enable them to regain control over their lives and find a way of living that is meaningful and satisfying to them. This approach foregrounds the importance of the social, and potentially fits well with the idea of self-directed support which is becoming central to the philosophy of social care.

Valuing evidence and evidence-based practice

Somewhat in contradiction to the valuing of service user and carer expertise has been the emergence of a particular version of evidence-based practice which has become dominant within medicine and which privileges certain forms of evidence over others. Within this, practitioners are expected just to apply a repertoire of standardised interventions that have been validated on the basis of Randomised Controlled Trials (RCTs). Evidence that relates to people's subjective experience or to the complex interactions between their inner world and their social situations can therefore be excluded from consideration (Tew et al., 2006).

While *evidence-based practice* can be helpful in some contexts in questioning practices which may be damaging and promoting alternatives that may be more effective, its somewhat over-zealous application may also have certain more damaging consequences in terms of:

- inviting practitioners (of all disciplines) to take on the role of a technical expert who can remain distant from any personal engagement with people's distress;
- avoiding the complexity of the whole person in their social situation and looking just for standardised solutions to simplified problems;
- bracketing out any consideration of social diversity and the impact of discrimination and cultural factors on mental health.

Clearly, the use of evidence is crucial in guiding practice. However, a social approach requires a more sophisticated use of evidence, one which includes sources such as personal narratives and longitudinal studies in order to tease out what may actually make a difference within the complexity of 'real-world' settings. Furthermore, evidence should not be imposed on people and their situations in order to come up with some formulaic response in terms of predefined interventions. Instead, it should be used to augment and develop the insights that people may already have into their situations – perhaps to explore why certain coping strategies may not be working and to suggest alternatives that might work better.

Box 1.1   The languages of biomedical and social models

Biomedical	Social
Mental illness	Mental distress
Symptom	Experience
Diagnosis	Meaning
Treatment	Action Planning
Cure	Empowerment
Care	Self-directed support

Interdisciplinary working and values-based practice

Professional values have a major influence, not just on how practitioners act and the decisions that they take, but, even more fundamentally, in how they perceive and interpret people's mental distress and their wider circumstances. Colombo et al. (2003) identified a range of implicit models of mental distress that were more or less prevalent across different professional groups, service users and carers. An apparent adherence to a biopsychosocial approach as an integrative framework can mask serious incompatibilities between the different theoretical orientations and fundamental ontological differences as to what is mental distress (see Chapter 2) – and social perspectives may often become subordinated within practice discourses that are dominated by a biomedical approach (Tew, 1999). This is exemplified in the tendency for medical rather than social forms of language to frame interdisciplinary case discussions – in ways that can easily invalidate the direct experience and perspectives of service users and carers (see Box 1.1).

Values-based practice involves making explicit our differences in values and language and how we perceive and interpret people's mental distress and their wider circumstances. Within this, it is important for social workers and other socially-minded practitioners to act as champions of social values and perspectives in multi-disciplinary teams. Such a championing must be within the spirit of an inclusive dialogue: the assertion of the social should not mean devaluing other perspectives, or trying to compete with other practitioners in a professional 'bubble' that excludes service users and carers.

Good practice involves centring the discussion on the unique experiences and perspectives of those who are living through a mental health difficulty: a core commitment to empathetic under-standing provides a sound (and ethical) basis for exploring the relevance and potential contribution of different professional val-ues.

Underpinning all elements of values-based practice are principles of dialogue and mutual respect – whether between practitioners, service users and carers or across professional disciplines. However, establishing this in practice is far from straightforward, given cur-rent inequalities in power and status between practitioners of differ-ent disciplines and between practitioners, service users and carers. Unless this is acknowledged and addressed within the discourses of multi-disciplinary teams, or in the discussions that take place with service users and carers in ward rounds or reviews, it can be hard to see how values-based practice can be more than rhetoric in many contexts. Nevertheless, it is an important aspiration which, if carried forward, has the potential to transform the culture of mental health services to one which is much more genuinely user and carer centred, and where different disciplinary perspectives may come together in creative ways. Achieving this requires developing practice skills such as awareness, reasoning and communication (Woodbridge and Fulford, 2004).

Core values for mental health practice

While there are clearly strengths in such a pluralist approach to values, there is also a danger that it leads to a lack of coherent focus within mental health services – or to implicit domination by one particular value system. This suggests the need for shared core values that would underpin the practice of all mental health practi-tioners – values that need to be driven by needs and aspirations of service users and carers rather than by the vested interests of professional groups.

Within the UK, the introduction of the Ten Essential Shared Capabilities (Box 1.2) provides a useful framework for starting to define what this core should be. Although it was not developed as a value base as such, it signals a shift in emphasis in mental health services away from a more traditional medical–clinical ethos to one which aims to be more socially and recovery-oriented, and one which values a 'doing with' rather than a 'doing to' style of working.

Box 1.2   The Ten Essential Shared Capabilities

The Ten Essential Shared Capabilities are:

1. **Working in Partnership**. Developing and maintaining constructive working relationships with service users, carers, families, colleagues, lay people and wider community networks. Working positively with any tensions created by conflict of interest or aspiration that may arise between the partners in care.

2. **Respecting Diversity**. Working in partnership with service users, carers, families and colleagues to provide care and interventions that not only make a positive difference but also do so in ways that respect and value diversity including age, race, culture, disability, gender, spirituality and sexuality.

3. **Practising Ethically**. Recognising the rights and aspirations of service users and their families, acknowledging power differentials and minimising them whenever possible. Providing treatment and care that is accountable to service users and carers within the boundaries prescribed by national (professional), legal and local codes of ethical practice.

4. **Challenging Inequality**. Addressing the causes and consequences of stigma, discrimination, social inequality and exclusion on service users, carers and mental health services. Creating, developing or maintaining valued social roles for people in the communities they come from.

5. **Promoting Recovery**. Working in partnership to provide care and treatment that enables service users and carers to tackle mental health problems with hope and optimism and to work towards a valued lifestyle within and beyond the limits of any mental health problem.

6. **Identifying People's Needs and Strengths**. Working in partnership to gather information to agree health and social care needs in the context of the preferred lifestyle and aspirations of service users, their families, carers and friends.

7. **Providing Service User Centred Care**. Negotiating achievable and meaningful goals; primarily from the perspective of service users and their families. Influencing and seeking the means to achieve these goals and clarifying the responsibilities of the people who will provide any help that is needed, including systematically evaluating outcomes and achievements.

8. **Making a Difference**. Facilitating access to and delivering the best quality, evidence-based, values-based health and social care interventions to meet the needs and aspirations of service users and their families and carers.

9. **Promoting Safety and Positive Risk Taking**. Empowering the person to decide the level of risk they are prepared to take with their health and safety. This includes working with the tension between promoting safety and positive risk taking, including assessing and dealing with possible risks for service users, carers, family members, and the wider public.

10. **Personal Development and Learning**. Keeping up to date with changes in practice and participating in life-long learning, personal and professional development for one's self and colleagues through supervision, appraisal and reflective practice.

Source: Department of Health (2004), *The Ten Essential Shared Capabilities: A Framework for the whole of the Mental Health Workforce*, London: Department of Health. Reproduced under Crown Copyright.

Recovery values and working relationships

As will be discussed in more detail in Chapter 9, the current concept of recovery is one that has emerged from the experiences of those who have gone through mental distress. It shifts the emphasis away from a medical discourse of symptom reduction to a more holistic perspective in which 'recovery' is seen as a journey of discovery and empowerment in which people reclaim valued identities and social roles, irrespective of whether they may continue to have certain unusual mental or emotional experiences. It also focuses on people's strengths and resources, rather than having a preoccupation with their 'deficits' and what they may (temporarily) be unable to do.

The implications of recovery are profound in terms of overturning conventional cultures, perceptions and attitudes within mental health services (Slade, 2009). It involves challenging the implicit message that runs through much of current service cultures to the effect that 'You will never be quite well again and we will do our best to look after you', and substituting a message of hope that 'You can change your situation and how you feel about yourself – and find your own ways of leading a meaningful and satisfying life.'

Recovery values have major implications in terms of the structuring of therapeutic relationships, transferring the locus of control from the practitioner to those dealing at first hand with their mental distress (see Box 1.3).

Box 1.3   Recovery values

- Working with a person is a privilege.
- Recovery practice values the ability for a person to be a locus of their own control.
- Recovery is a mutual and equal process.
- Recovery values 'use of self'.
- Recovery espouses validation of experiences.
- Finding meaning, and a reason to recover or change, is integral to the recovery process.
- Recovery acknowledges the value of helpful relationships and connections
- Recovery practice demonstrates hope.
- Recovery practice values the skill of balancing when to do for someone, do with someone, or support them to do for themselves.
- Recovery involves the challenge and extension of comfort boundaries.
- Recovery outcomes are individual and cannot be predetermined.

Source: Glover, 2003.

Getting alongside people who are experiencing mental distress is not always easy. They may be frightened, confused or distrustful – and aspects of what they say or how they are acting may be hard to understand on first encounter. Being guided by some basic values and orientations may make all the difference between establishing the basis for a partnership that will support someone towards recovery, and (however inadvertently) taking on a position of professional superiority that may be fundamentally disempowering and may serve to trap people within mental health services.

Constructing relationships on the basis of 'care' or 'treatment' can be problematic as this can tend to imply a model of 'doing to' which presumes an ongoing polarity between a superior person who possesses competence and expertise, and a relatively passive (and potentially inferiorised) person who receives the help that they are given. Thus, however useful the care or treatment may be in the short term, it may carry with it a very powerful message that takes away control and responsibility and invites the person to see themselves as a 'patient' who must wait for others to sort out their mental distress for them.

Alternative approaches which fit better with a recovery orientation are 'doing with' and 'being alongside'. 'Doing with' implies an active partnership with a shared responsibility for setting the direction. 'Being alongside' takes the shift in power and control even further and situates the person experiencing mental distress in the 'driving seat', with the worker as facilitator, ally and supporter – a shift in orientation and power dynamics that may be quite challenging to those used to more traditional professional roles:

> The challenge within recovery focused practice is to 'be alongside' as service users take the lead in constructing their own recovery journey ... [This] goes against our human and professional instincts to 'help' or 'sort out problems', particularly when someone is experiencing distress. Taking a step back from this more active role takes skill and patience and requires us to have trust in, and respect for, the service users we work with. It is only through demonstrating this faith in the individuals we work with that they in turn will develop confidence in their own abilities to manage the situations that they find themselves in. (Alexander, 2008, p. 21)

Models for working relationships, such as coaching and mentoring, which have been imported from fields such as adult education and sport science, can offer more of an ethos of equality between service provider and service user, and can give the service user a greater sense of control over the terms of the working relationship (Green et al., 2006). These are proving both more acceptable to service users and more effective in terms of supporting people's recovery – and people with their own lived experience of mental distress can often find that they have something special to offer in such roles.

Nevertheless, many professionals can remain locked into an approach which is founded on maintaining superiority and distance – playing the role of an 'expert' who can assess a situation and decide which of a range of pre-designed and validated interventions should be applied. However, the evidence shows that what actually makes the difference in promoting recovery is not so much the effectiveness of particular techniques as the quality of working relationships (Gilbert and Leahy, 2007; Keijsers et al., 2000; Schon et al., 2009). It is a human-to-human relationship that can provide the acceptance, affirmation, respect and connection which can be key to reclaiming one's identity and place in the world (Holley, 2007). Such a relationship can only work on the basis of a working partnership which is not skewed by differences of power and status, and where practitioners can be open about their feelings and experience, and allow themselves to be moved emotionally by what people may express to them.

A value base for a social approach

Using the Ten Essential Shared Capabilities and recovery values as starting points, and drawing upon some of the practice values of social work, we may develop a statement of the values and orientations that are central to a social approach to mental health practice. These include:

Working collaboratively

Although there can be many attempts to dilute the meaning of 'partnership' within services that have traditionally been organised along hierarchical lines, a partnership approach overturns cultures of professional superiority that are grounded in 'us' and 'them' thinking. Instead, it foregrounds the importance of mutuality and respect within therapeutic relationships and links with the idea of co-production in which outcomes are achieved collaboratively by pooling resources and expertise (Needham and Carr, 2009). This has major implications in terms of how we approach areas such as safeguarding, assessment and Action Planning.

Respecting diversity and challenging forms of oppression

This involves recognising the degree to which discrimination and disadvantage may both contribute to people's mental distress and result in their unfair treatment within mental health services – and making a commitment to ensure that differences in identity are valued and forms of oppression are challenged (Dominelli, 2002; Thompson, 2006).

Empowerment, inclusion and citizenship

Emancipatory practice involves enabling people to reclaim control over their lives, direct their own support and become more confident in developing positive forms of power for themselves (Braye and Preston-Shoot, 1995). Beyond this, it also involves enabling them to become involved, as full and equal citizens, in whatever aspects of mainstream society that they choose (Sayce, 2000).

This suggests an orientation towards practice which is as much about promoting social change as it is about enabling individual recovery. It is also implies a profoundly democratic approach in which knowledge and information is shared and people are given the tools they need in order to direct and achieve their own recovery.

Looking for meaning

It is important to start with the assumption that all expressions of mental distress are ways in which we may be trying to express 'the meaning of our lives' (Plumb, 1999, p. 471). So, instead of writing them off as 'symptoms' of a 'mental illness', distress experiences should be respected and taken seriously as an attempt to communicate something – perhaps about an injustice or a 'problem of living' – which may be very hard to express by more conventional means.

Seeing the person-in-context

A social approach privileges a systemic rather than a reductionist way of viewing distress: it aims to see a person *in relationship with* their social and cultural context, rather than seeking to abstract a specific symptom or disease entity that can be treated in isolation. Their wider social situation and their inner experiences are equally important – and inextricably linked.

Over and above these specific values, other more general professional values are important within mental health work, such as honesty, integrity and respect for individuality and personal dignity. In some (often quite limited) situations there can be an overriding duty to protect those who may be vulnerable or in danger. However, more often, it can be important for practitioners to take a step back from this position, with its implications of professional authority over others, in order to be alongside people as they struggle to resolve their difficulties in their own way – which is likely to involve an element of *positive* risk-taking (see Chapter 10).

Summary of key points

- Personal and professional values shape the ways in which we see the world and our ways of relating to others.
- Discussing differences in values are important if wwe are to work collaboratively with others (*values-based practice*).
- Working relationships that are effective in supporting recovery are based on:
  - 'being alongside' rather than 'doing to';
  - developing human-to-human personal relationships;
  - valuing service users and carers as experts by experience.
- The value base for a social approach emphasises:
  - working collaboratively;
  - respecting diversity and challenging forms of oppression;
  - empowerment, inclusion and citizenship;
  - looking for meaning in people's experiences;
  - seeing the person-in-context.

Further reading

Exploring values and practice:
Woodbridge, K., & Fulford, K. (2004). *Whose Values? A Workbook for Values-Based Practice in Mental Health Care*. London: Sainsbury Centre for Mental Health.

Putting socially oriented values and capabilities into practice:
Stickley, T., & Bassett, T. (eds) (2008). *Learning About Mental Health Practice*. Chichester: Wiley, Chapters 3–11.

2 | Understanding the experience of mental distress

In this chapter, I will review how we should understand mental health and mental distress (and how we distinguish the latter from everyday upset and discontent) with a particular focus on non-medical and service user perspectives. Rather than conceptualising mental distress as a disease, it may more helpful to view it as a meaningful response to adverse social experiences and problems of living.

Mental health, wellbeing and everyday life

Defining positive mental health is not straightforward, as this can be highly subjective and there can be profound social and cultural differences in how it might be understood. Individualised definitions can focus on a person's social adjustment and functioning, their emotional vitality and self-esteem, and their ability to 'work productively and fruitfully and [be] able to make a contribution to his or her community' (World Health Organisation, 2001, p. 1). However, such definitions fail to take account of their social context: to what they are being asked to adjust, and what opportunities may they actually have to be productive or make valued contributions to their community?

This suggests the need for our understanding of mental wellbeing to embrace, not just aspects of our inner life and outward behaviour, but also the quality of our social relationships and connections, our ability to access positive identities and statuses, and our social experiences of fairness, inclusion, respect and opportunity. This requires us to consider, not just the mental wellbeing of individuals, but also the mental wellbeing of relationship systems such as families, peer groups, communities and societies as a whole.

Within advanced countries, there is a clear negative correlation between income inequalities and overall mental wellbeing. Societies characterised by inequality, status competition and 'in-your-face' relative deprivation are deleterious to the mental health not only of those who are disadvantaged or excluded, but also of those who are apparently prospering as a result of these divisive social relations (Wilkinson, 2005). This perspective needs to be extended to include other forms of discrimination – such as racism or homophobia – so that our understanding of a mentally healthy social context would be one characterised by collaborative and inclusive social relations and a valuing of diverse identities.

Mental wellbeing may be seen to comprise two distinct aspects:

- subjective experience of happiness, pleasure and contentment; and
- social engagement and personal efficacy. (Ryan and Deci, 2001)

In his analysis of the economic costs of mental distress, Richard Layard proposed 'happiness' as a political and economic objective – instead of simply pursuing wealth creation as an end in itself (Layard, 2006). While the equation of mental health with happiness may be somewhat one-dimensional, the work of the Positive Psychology movement (upon which Layard draws) offers a somewhat broader vision of mental health which includes, not just the capacity to experience *positive emotions*, but also *engagement* in relationships and activities, and having a subjective sense that life has *meaning* or purpose (Duckworth et al., 2005). These are themes that we will return to in our discussion of resilience (in Chapter 5) and recovery (in Chapter 9).

What can be missing from a focus on wellbeing is an acknowledgement of the less pleasant aspects of ordinary life – from boredom and frustration through to conflict and loss. It is important that experiences of upset and discontent, and the emotions of anger, sadness or fear that may go with them, are nevertheless seen as part of a mentally healthy life. It is by working through these experiences that we grow, move on and make changes in the world in which we live. This suggests an important conceptual difference between positive mental health and mental wellbeing: mental health does *not* imply some state of perpetual happiness or satisfaction. However, there has been an emerging tendency within developed societies to expect a life that is somehow free of risk or adversity, with a hedonistic right to experience constant pleasure. This has led to an increasing discomfort with 'difficult' feelings such as anxiety, rage or grief, and a tendency to medicalise them within a spectrum of mental 'illness', rather than seeing them as healthy and natural responses to difficult or challenging situations.

Rather than conceptualise positive mental health as a 'state' with which we may or may not be endowed, it may be more helpful to see it as a *process* – one that is generated and reproduced through positive interactions between the personal and the social. It may be self-sustaining as a 'virtuous circle', but it is also vulnerable to the possibility of disruption. If a link in the circle becomes broken for whatever reason, the process may break down, and the virtuous circle be replaced by a downward and self-reinforcing spiral of disconnection and distress.

Antisocial behaviour: mental distress or moral deviance?

A particular area of confusion in both public and professional discourses around violence and criminality is whether people should be treated as 'mad' or 'bad':

> The portrayal of the mentally ill is always that they are threatening [and] there is always the association of crime and mental illness, as if people need this as an explanation for people having done awful things' (service user, quoted in Foster, 2007, p. 105).

In recent years, there has been an increasing tendency to use 'mental illness' as an explanation for behaviour that is deviant or anti-social – bringing the regulation of criminality increasingly within the sphere of psychiatry. This is both undermining of the notion of moral responsibility – people with mental distress have the same moral responsibilities as other citizens – and has contributed to the unfortunate conflation in the public (and sometimes the professional) mind of mental distress with a propensity to violence. In turn, this association has led to the increasing stigmatisation of people experiencing mental distress (Sayce, 2000).

There is the danger of a circular logic in which a 'repetitive and persistent pattern of behaviour in which the rights of others or major age-appropriate societal norms or rules are violated' becomes an essential defining criterion of a medical diagnosis of 'anti-social personality disorder' (American Psychiatric Association, 1994). This diagnosis is then used, tautologically, to 'explain' the very same patterns of behaviour and deviant lifestyles which constitute its definition – and thereby to suggest a psychiatric rather than a criminological basis for managing any risk of violence or anti-social behaviour.

While such an orientation towards life may potentially be distressing towards others, it does not necessarily correlate with any inner turmoil, confusion or other sign of mental distress. Primarily, it raises legal and moral issues. It also raises gender issues, since offenders are more often male, and certain elements of such orientations fit well with expectations around male socialisation (Featherstone et al., 2007). It is probably more helpful that such behaviour, and the attitudes and values that underlie it, are responded to within the arenas of criminal justice and community safety. Invoking a psychiatric discourse can potentially offer an excuse that allows offenders to evade their moral responsibilities while providing no significant 'added value' in terms of treatment strategies.

The legal process allows for 'out-of-character' instances of violence or threatening behaviour, where a person may be taken to have 'diminished responsibility' due to their mental or emotional state – perhaps due to fear of attack or passionate jealousy in response to an infidelity, or intoxication due to drugs or alcohol. Experiences of mental distress can simply take their place alongside these as potential factors to be taken into account – without the need to switch into a psychiatric discourse of explanation. As will be discussed in Chapter 10, there is very little overall correlation between any psychiatric 'illness' diagnosis and an enhanced propensity for violence.

Where people undertake criminal behaviour *and also* experience mental distress, this does not necessarily imply that the mental distress is the *cause* of it – and the commonly held assumptions around such causal connections may be seen as outdated (Hollin, 1997). People have choices as to how they respond to unusual mental or emotional experiences – and both mental distress and criminality may both be responses to certain underlying common factors such as poverty, living in disorganised neighbourhoods, drug use, family breakdown, and so on – but may operate relatively independently of one another. Research would also indicate that a well established pattern of criminality or anti-social behaviour in later adolescence may connect with a higher propensity for psychotic breakdown in later life (Hodgins and Müller-Isberner, 2004) – suggesting that such a lifestyle and its consequences (such as imprisonment) may be a significant contributory factor towards later mental distress. Thus, while it is important not to conflate mental distress with a higher propensity to commit criminal acts, it is also important to recognise that a substantial proportion of those being dealt with by the criminal justice system may also have mental health needs.

Cultural perspectives

Our experiences of mental distress are constituted in relation to our specific historic and cultural context. It is this that provides a framework of meanings, symbols, concerns and modes of expression that forms the backdrop against which specific experiences of mental distress are constructed and played out. For example, during the Cold War, people in the West would frequently attach their heightened fears and anxieties to a belief that they were being spied on or faced imminent attack from the Russians. Other experiences of mental distress may be articulated using images and themes from systems of religious belief: people may identify themselves as a prophet or possessed by a spirit.

Cultural context may be important in defining what is or is not to be seen as an experience of mental distress (Fernando, 2010). In some contexts, hearing the voice of God or of an ancestor may be seen as a highly prized spiritual experience; in others this may lead to compulsory admission to psychiatric hospital. Experiences of mental distress – whether more florid psychosis or more mundane depression – may be seen as situated on the margins of what is acceptable and comprehensible within a specific cultural context, challenging and sometimes transgressing systems of meaning and expectation.

Many ethnic communities are experiencing relatively rapid cultural change and people may have to construct themselves in relation to coexisting traditional and Westernised frames of reference. Research has shown how people may hold a number of parallel conceptions about mental distress. While it may be understood as an illness or as a response to social adversity, it may also be seen in more traditional ways as caused by:

- punishment for wrongdoings;
- shame and bringing the family and community into disrepute;
- possession by spirits and demons. (Glasgow Anti-Stigma Partnership, 2007).

Increasingly there may be a need for 'cultural consultancy' – an anthropological approach that seeks to bring together the very different cultural life-worlds of service users and mental health practitioners (Kilshaw et al., 2002).

Medical diagnosis and the biologising of mental distress

For most of the twentieth century, the dominant language for conceptualising experiences of mental distress was the biomedical approach, which has defined them as if they were the symptoms of hypothetical illnesses or impairments. However, after nearly a century of well-funded research, the evidence for consistent illness processes (pathologies) 'taking over' a person is still as tentative as it ever was (Bentall, 2004). The exception to this has been our understanding of the biology of degenerative brain diseases, such as dementia or Huntington's Chorea, which result in a somewhat different range of experiences, including memory loss and cognitive impairment, that are outside the scope of this book.

While a holistic approach to mental distress implies a coming together of social, psychological and medical perspectives – the 'Biopsychosocial' Model – there remains a fundamental dualism between mind and body that is hard to bridge. In seeking to comprehend mental distress, are we exploring complex but potentially meaningful personal experiences, or are we talking about symptoms arising from diseases of the brain (albeit ones which may be triggered by adverse social circumstances)? Each perspective implies a radically different ontology – a fundamentally differing conception of what it is that needs to be understood.

Early in the twentieth century, the philosopher and psychiatrist Karl Jaspers (1913) proposed a distinction between forms of distress that were:

- potentially comprehensible, if one could put oneself into the other's life situation; or
- so strange and apparently unconnected with life experience that they went beyond the bounds of empathetic understanding.

The latter were to be explained as resulting from chemical imbalances or other biological processes affecting the brain – even in the absence of any direct evidence of such processes taking place. This led to the later custom-and-practice definition of a psychiatric symptom as something 'with which the examiner cannot empathise' (Fish, 1966, p. 270).

The 'biologising' of apparently incomprehensible experience was taken forward as a dominant tradition within the development of twentieth-century psychiatry. In this, the clinician is instructed to ignore the content of people's experience in favour of categorising the specific type of experience so as to confirm (or refute) a particular diagnosis. Thus it would be seen as important whether a person believed that others were inserting thoughts into their head – but irrelevant what the thoughts were and who might be seen as inserting them.

Central to this project has been the postulating of specific mental 'illnesses' – such as 'schizophrenia' and 'bipolar disorder' – which would each be characterised by a consistent set of symptoms (types of distress experience). However, as a system of classification, the evidence for particular sets of symptoms clustering together as specific 'illnesses' is very weak (Bentall, 2004). Although they may be presented as taken-for-granted facts within mainstream psychiatric discourse, medical diagnoses such as 'schizophrenia' do not stand up well as scientifically reliable constructs (Boyle, 2002). The variations of people's experiences are such that there is no common core of symptoms that consistently correlate with one another in a way that separates out one 'illness' from another.

As well as having somewhat dubious scientific validity, such diagnoses have limited practical utility. A particular diagnosis does not provide a clear guide as to the level of someone's need or dysfunction – someone with a 'severe' diagnosis such as schizophrenia may be able to hold down a job and have a high quality of family life, whereas someone with a less 'serious' diagnosis, such as depression, may be completely incapacitated. Despite popular misconceptions, diagnosis has no reliable predictive value in relation to risk (see Chapter 10). Nor is it helpful in indicating people's potential for recovery – for example, in terms of their readiness to complete a vocational training programme (Tsang et al., 2000).

Nevertheless, over recent years, and particularly during the 'decade of the brain' in the 1990s, a biological perspective has achieved a position of pre-eminence within the practical application of the Biopsychosocial Model (see Figure 2.1).

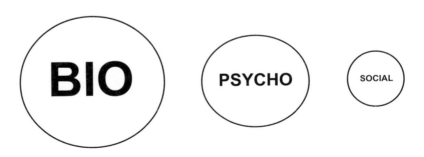

Figure 2.1 The Biopsychosocial Model in relation to current mental health practice

> **Box 2.1 'A bolt out of the blue'**
>
> A person is hit by a biochemical event that
> impacts on how they think, feel and behave
> and has implications for their family life, employment, housing
> needs …
>
> So, if doctors treat the illness, the rest will sort itself out
> (with some help and support).
>
> However, if they do not get better, then they have a chronic
> illness and will always need looking after.

It was presumed that social or psychological factors played only a subsidiary role in triggering an underlying mental 'illness' – and, by implication, had a similarly subsidiary role as an adjunct to medical interventions in its treatment. This resulted in dominant way of understanding mental distress within both lay and professional discourses, which may be characterised as 'A bolt out of the blue' (see Box 2.1). This discourse effectively disconnects the meaning of people's distress from any relationship with their life experience, and renders them powerless to influence its course.

Re-visioning the relationship between the biological and the social

If the whole concept of 'illness' may be seen to be both scientifically unsubstantiated and often unhelpful as a metaphor by which to conceptualise distress, then the basis of the interrelationship between social, personal and biological factors needs to be revisited.

A rejection of the disease model of 'mental illness' does not imply that the biological dimension is unimportant. Far from it. However, a different model of causality may be required. Instead of some underlying illness being seen as the cause, and experiences of mental distress as symptoms, we are gaining increasing evidence that trauma and other adverse life experiences make their imprint on our physiology and biochemistry – and developments in brain-imaging technology are demonstrating just how much brain functioning may change in response to such experiences (Perry et al., 1995; Shonkoff and Phillips, 2000). In this way, the social can be the underlying cause *both* of problematic cognitive, emotional and behavioural responses *and* of associated biochemical and physiological changes. Alongside this, new experiences – either arising through therapy or exposure to more positive social situations – can lead to positive changes in brain functioning (Roffman et al., 2005). In this way, new and better life experiences can start to undo the biological legacy of adverse experience.

Similarly, a rejection of the disease model does not take away from the possibility that genetics or other physical factors may affect our abilities to deal with particular forms of stress – although this is very different from being able to identify a 'schizophrenia' gene that can be transmitted down the generations. While longitudinal research in Finland has indicated that, on their own, the effect of an adverse environment is much greater than genetics as a contributory factor towards subsequent breakdown, the combination of both was found to be particularly pernicious in its longer-term impact (Tienari et al., 2004; see Chapter 6).

Nor does moving away from the 'illness' model of mental distress take away from the possibility that psychoactive medication can have specific effects (for example to tranquillise, to raise mood, or to distance a person from their emotions) which may or may not be helpful to people if they are experiencing mental distress. However, despite the impression created by pharmaceutical advertising, their action is not about targeting and curing particular 'illness' processes; instead they may be seen to act on anyone, irrespective of diagnosis, as do other psychoactive drugs such as sleeping pills or alcohol (Moncrieff, 2008). Thus, a revisioning of medical approaches would suggest that 'medication could be better targeted at problems and processes rather than putative "illnesses" ' (Kinderman et al., 2008) – and the fact that someone may find medication helpful in enabling them to deal with their mental experience would not imply that they are suffering from any underlying brain disease.

Such a re-visioning of the relationship between the biological and the social removes the unhelpful and simplistic dualism between 'normal' and 'psychopathological' experience – and the construction of categories of 'us' and 'them' that follow on from it – as everyone's brain chemistry can both evolve in response to, and influence, their life experience. Out of this, there emerges the possibility of a more sophisticated approach in which all manifestations of mental distress may be understood as part of a continuum of potentially understandable responses to challenging life situations. While each distress response may have its physiological manifestations and consequences (so that medication or other physical treatments may potentially be helpful), its content should be taken seriously as a potential expression of meaning in relation to people's life experience and social circumstances:

There is no logical inconsistency in believing that one's distress has been precipitated by socio-political factors and taking medication to control one's natural or learned responses to these events. In principle, this is no different from taking paracetamol to ease the pain of a headache due to overtiredness. The problem arises when the belief that one's distress has been provoked by socio-political circumstances is denied, ridiculed or invalidated. (Coppock and Hopton, 2000, p. 160)

Reclaiming meaning: learning from those with lived experience

Although critically minded practitioners from a range of professional backgrounds have sought to keep the debate open as to how forms of mental distress should be understood, it has been the service user movement which has been most influential in driving current debates about its nature and meaning (Hammersley and McLaughlin, 2006; Wallcraft and Michaelson, 2001). Diagnostic labels such as 'schizophrenic' can have major implications in terms of stigmatisation and social status, and what may start as a diagnosis may take over and come to define people's identities – see Chapter 7.

In Britain and elsewhere, people are beginning to claim and construct their own definitions of their experiences (Geekie, 2004). Perhaps the most influential example of this has been the Hearing Voices Network in which people have come together as peers to develop and share their understanding of voice-hearing experiences (Hornstein, 2009). A focus on the phenomenology of their actual experience, rather than any diagnosis, has been crucial in empowering people to grapple with what such experiences may mean to them and what may be their most effective strategies to work with and respond to what their voices may be saying. Joining the Network has enabled many people to reclaim their identities as no longer passive victims of a medical condition but as active human beings who (sometimes) hear voices and have their own ways of dealing with any distress that may arise from this.

An important message from people with lived experience is that we should not always see unusual mental experiences as inherently 'bad' and in need of eradication – as has been the implication of a biomedical approach. People who have mood swings or hear voices may also describe aspects of such experiences as being a valuable part of who they are – although they may also present them with challenges and difficulties. Sometimes people may identify a 'symptom' such as self-harm as their best available survival strategy within current circumstances.

For many people, mental distress can involve a deep sense of disconnection – both from aspects of oneself and from one's social and physical environment (Hutton, 2008). For some people, it can involve deep uncertainties about the meaning and significance of events, relationships and even familiar objects:

> I stand alone, unable to move inside a dark bubble. I have no face or hands or feet. My veins are broken and my blood has nowhere to travel. Outside the bubble is day. A rainbow appears but I cannot see it. I remain in the bubble, broken and hidden from the life around me. (O'Hagan, 2009, p. 199)

Much of the taken-for-granted world can become problematised or seen in new ways. Distrust or rejection of conventional frames of meaning can lead to a person 'dropping out' of mainstream discourse and language – which can be intensely isolating. In some instances, manifestations of distress may be understood as desperate and unconventional attempts at communicating where there may seem to be no available language in which the person can express what their unease is about (Lefevre, 1996).

Perhaps one of the most powerful perspectives to have emerged out of people's lived experience of recovery is to see experiences of mental distress as a journey: sometimes a journey that eventually brings people back to somewhere near their starting point, but more often a transformative journey – a process of discovery that may eventually lead to new self-understandings, identities and lifestyle choices (Deegan, 1996). This perspective provides an antithesis to the tendency for mental distress to be represented as a chronic 'illness', characterised by inevitable and ongoing deterioration – a vision that has led many people to feel helpless and hopeless, and sometimes suicidal.

Changing the metaphor: from disease to unease

Whereas the notion of 'disease' suggests a biological process that invades and takes us over, Thomas Szasz (1961) suggests that we view manifestations of mental distress as extreme but potentially meaningful responses to 'problems of living' that involve both our inner and our external worlds. Therefore, rather than seeking to understand mental distress as a medical *dis-ease,* it may be more helpful to see it as arising out of a state of *un-ease* both with ourselves and our wider social situation. In many situations, we may be able to resolve our unease for ourselves – perhaps through making changes in our lives or through dealing with unresolved issues that are troubling us. In other instances, we may (just about) be able to hold our unease inside while putting on a 'normal' face to the wider world. However, at some point, this unease may start to come back to the surface, particularly if current life circumstances may be stressful or difficult. If we cannot contain or deal with our unease, this may escalate to the point where it becomes mental distress (see Chapter 7).

If we abandon the vocabulary of 'illness', we need an alternative language whereby to describe different sorts of distress experiences. Richard Bentall (2003) suggests that we use the straightforwardly descriptive language of *complaints* – what is the specific experience that is troubling us? So, instead of being diagnosed with 'schizophrenia', we might simply describe ourselves as having a difficulty in managing an abusive internal voice, or a fixed belief that we are being followed – and any therapeutic help would be targeted at resolving the specific complaint, rather than treating a supposed underlying illness.

Social approaches to understanding mental distress

Mental distress involves a disordering or breakdown of aspects of emotional, mental and social functioning such that we may no longer fit in with the accepted norms of our social and cultural context. Although, subjectively, experiences can seem very different, what is perhaps the defining characteristic of all forms of mental distress is the disruption of our *personal agency*: our ability or organise ourselves sufficiently in order to deal either with our underlying unease or the ordinary expectations of our social and family lives. We may see ourselves as being 'all over the place' – and particular thoughts, feelings or behaviours may 'take us over', acquiring a momentum and direction of their own and pushing us to act and relate in ways that may be unfamiliar or scary.

If we move beyond seeing manifestations of mental distress as the 'symptoms' of an underlying disease process, there are two ways of looking at mental distress that may be particularly useful in making sense of the experience. Building upon what Judith Herman (1997) has proposed as the 'central dialectic' of psychological trauma, any manifestation of mental distress may (somewhat paradoxically) be seen as *both*:

- A way of coping with (or containing) our underlying unease; *and*
- A 'cry for help' that may also express (often indirectly) what the unease may be about.

As a coping strategy, it may need to be respected as our best available way of holding in our unease, or trying to carry on within what has become for us an unliveable social situation. It may involve an escalation of familiar strategies which may have worked well in the past, or it may involve recourse to more extreme or unusual ways of coping or trying to protect ourselves. While this may be at considerable cost to ourselves (and others), it may nevertheless constitute our only way of containing the experience, or problem of living, that we feel we cannot face directly.

In parallel with this, manifestations of distress may also be seen as a way of signalling just how unliveable our current situation may be:

> I am a long piercing scream.
> All screaming on the inside of me
> and out of the pores of my skin.
> My screaming and myself are one.
> This is pure pain.
> (O'Hagan, 2009, p. 200)

They may also call attention to a difficult experience that we may (consciously or unconsciously) be holding inside. The particular form taken by the distress may provide clues as to the issues that may underlie it. It may sometimes represent a spilling out of aspects of our experience (for example, our sexual orientation) that do not fit easily within the constraints of the 'normal' identities we may be expected to perform. It may allude to the oppressiveness of our social situation, or the abusiveness of certain relationships (past or present). It may signal tensions or crises within our families or other key relationship systems – or a sense of loss or abandonment.

Although some expressions of mental distress present as relatively straightforward responses to recent life events of circumstances – for example, feeling depressed following an experience of loss – many mental health crises, and the issues that underlie them, tend to be complex and multi-faceted. If what may be starting to spill out is seen (both by the person and by those around) as unacceptable or shameful, what may emerge may appear detached or coded. Any attempt at understanding may require us to go beyond the limits of 'common sense' (Ingleby, 1981), as they may reveal multiple layers of meaning and may need to be understood in a range of different (and potentially contradictory) ways. Within this, priority always needs to be given to helping a person to find their own meanings and make their own connections.

Different experiences of mental distress

While, as we have seen, processes of diagnosis may be unhelpful, it may nevertheless be useful to give a brief overview of different sorts of distress experience or complaint. Breakdown is never total, and some areas of functioning may be more affected than others – so actual complaints may be quite specific.

Emotional difficulties and mood swings

People may describe losing their emotional balance in different ways. Some people become locked in to a particular feeling state, such as anxiety or depression, which takes over and starts to exclude other emotions, leaving them with little capacity to be in emotional contact with the world around them. Other people may find that they swing between moods (such as depression and euphoria) or experience volatile or 'brittle' emotions which seem to bear little connection with current reality.

Such processes of emotional distortion may be exaggerations of everyday coping strategies but may also signify that, in some sense, it has all become 'too much'. For example, depression involves a closing down of emotional awareness and activity – which may make sense as a way of protecting oneself against inner pain and/or external pressures that cannot be faced. It may also represent a cry for help – although, paradoxically, the very process of closing down may render the person harder to reach in terms of negotiating or receiving support.

Psychosis, dissociation and confusing realities

The term psychosis may be used to describe a range of experiences that include:

- feeling over-stimulated and unable to control (or discriminate between) a bombardment of sensations;
- intense mental creativity and the making of original or unusual connections between ideas, perceptions and experiences;
- a sense that one's thoughts or actions are being controlled by others;
- irrational beliefs that are firmly held and not easily amenable to reason – and may involve paranoia or suspicion;
- using metaphoric or symbolic forms of communication to express experiences that cannot (safely) be expressed in everyday language.

Dissociation involves splitting off from aspects of internal experience or external reality and is generally understood as a response to trauma. Both psychosis and dissociation may involve feeling disconnected from anything that resembles a stable core sense of self.

Although potentially rather strange and disconcerting, some of these experiences may actually be quite similar to artistic creativity, spiritual experiences and other states of heightened sensitivity. Similarly, 'delusional' beliefs may not seem so unusual if we recognise that nearly everyone makes sense of their world by holding some 'irrational' beliefs – and some of these may be held with considerable conviction (such as religious beliefs). A recent community survey found 17.5% of the general population reported psychotic experiences (Van Os et al., 2000) whereas under 1% would have a formal diagnosis of mental illness. This indicates a continuum of experiences which, for the majority of people, are manageable and may be experienced as positive, but, for a minority, can be very troubling and interfere with their everyday life.

Hearing voices and other hallucinatory experiences

A more specific experience, which may or may not be related to other forms of psychotic experience, is that of hearing one or more internal voices that may speak to us – or sometimes to each other. This may represent a variant of inner dialogue or 'talking to oneself' – and it is suggested that 'people hear hallucinated voices when they misattribute their own inner speech to a source that is external or alien to themselves' (Bentall, 2004, p. 198). Sometimes people report visual hallucinations, smells or other tactile experiences – although these more frequently link to physical causes such as drugs or fever.

Internal voices may be those of familiar people, or their identities may be obscure. Typically voices 'say things that are especially relevant for the person hearing them and usually are related to ... an unresolved problem in daily life, (Romme and Escher, 2000, p. 36). Some people find what voices have to say can be helpful or comforting – the voice may be a 'spirit guide' who provides advice or useful information. However, around 25% of voice hearers can find the experience very frightening and disorientating, especially if the voices become overly critical or abusive (Pennings and Romme, 2000):

> I tried to confront the voice of Janet hoping it would stop tormenting me but it went on and on and on and on. Janet was alternating between sexually provocative behaviour and criticism directed

towards me ... It got to the point where I could no longer cope with the number of voices and their intensity and their ferocity. (Hill, 2008, p. 85)

Probably the hardest voices to live with are those that seem to have the power to command a person to do things that they would otherwise not do, including acts of self-harm or violence to others.

In addition, people's attempts to cope with voices or other hallucinations may themselves become problematic – they may exhibit disturbed concentration, apparently inappropriate expressions of emotion or socially isolating behaviours – and these patterns of response may need to be seen as part of their overall difficulty.

Self-harm and 'acting out' distress

Self-harm may involve a broad range of actions by which we act out our distress on ourselves, from over- or under-eating, through misusing substances, to more overt behaviours such as self-poisoning or self-injury. Alternatively, we may project our distress outwards onto others – perhaps through acts of aggression or abuse. Typically, men may have more opportunities to externalise their distress, whereas women (and children) may more often tend to take their distress out upon themselves.

People describe experiences of self-injury and self-harm in very different ways. For some, it involves substituting a controlled form of pain to mask an otherwise unbearable feeling or memory. For others, it is in response to a dissociative state of numbness where all feelings and sensations seem absent and the person is left doubting that they are still human or real. Either way, the act of self-harm may be seen as a way of regaining some control, but at very obvious cost to the person and sometimes also to their personal relationships.

When does an everyday experience turn into mental distress?

As we have seen, many experiences of mental distress tend to be extensions or exacerbations of everyday experiences or coping strategies – so the onset of distress may simply be a point along a continuum at which someone's experiences start seriously to interfere with their life. In determining whether a particular experience or pattern of response has reached the threshold where it has become a complaint of mental distress, we may need to consider:

1. Does a person feel predominantly in control of their thoughts, feelings or behaviour, or have some of these taken on a momen-

tum of their own, taking over and starting to control them as a person (*disruption of personal agency*)?

2. To what degree is the experience interfering with a person's ability to carry on with their daily life (*social dysfunction*)?

3. Has the escalation of a particular aspect of experience put the person or others in danger of harm or exploitation (*significant risk*)?

While most people will experience a disruption of personal agency that causes them problems in everyday functioning, not everyone will be at any significant degree of risk (particularly if they have good family or social support). Such criteria may be of much more practical value than medical diagnosis in assessing how a person – and their social situation – may be affected by their mental distress (see Chapter 11).

Summary of key points

- Mental wellbeing is more than subjective happiness – it involves social engagement and affirmative rather than oppressive social relationships.
- It is not helpful to treat everyday unhappiness – or criminal or anti-social behaviour – as a form of mental distress.
- The relationship between the social and the physiological needs to be rethought, given the evidence that social experiences can affect brain function.
- Instead of seeing mental distress as an 'illness', it may be more helpful to see it as an escalation of *unease* related to problems of living.
- An experience of mental distress can represent both:
  - an extreme strategy to *protect* ourselves from, or *cope* with, our underlying unease;
  - a way of *expressing* (often indirectly) what the unease may be about.
- *Complaints* of mental distress are varied and may include:
  - emotional difficulties and mood swings;
  - psychotic and dissociative experiences
  - hearing voices;
  - self-harm and 'acting out' one's distress.
- The point at which such experiences start to constitute a complaint of mental distress depends on the degree of

- ○ disruption of personal agency – where some aspects of one's experience seem 'out of control';
- ○ social dysfunction and impact on everyday life;
- ○ risk to self or others.

Further reading

First-person accounts of experiences:
Reynolds, J., Muston, R., Heller, T., Leach, J., McCormick, M., Wallcraft, J., & Walsh, M. (eds) (2009). *Mental Health Still Matters*. Basingstoke: Palgrave Macmillan.
See also Chipmunka publications (www.chipmunkapublishing.com).

More academic approaches to making sense of mental distress include:
Bentall, R. (2003). *Madness Explained: Psychosis and Human Nature* London: Penguin.
Read, J., Mosher, L., & Bentall, R. (eds) (2004). *Models of Madness*. Hove: Brunner–Routledge.

Practical workbooks to enable people to start making sense of their own experiences include:
Coleman, R., & Smith, M. (1997). *Working With Voices: From Victim to Victor*. Gloucester: Handsell.

3 | Social circumstances and life events: how damaging social experiences may contribute to mental distress

There is overwhelming evidence that both our wider social environment and particular life events, such as trauma or abuse, can play a major part in influencing whether we come to experience mental distress at some point in our lives. It is not only our current situation that makes a difference; it is also the cumulative impact of our previous social experience. In this chapter, I will review the growing evidence around the sorts of social experiences that may be potentially damaging to our mental health. As will be discussed in more depth in Chapter 4, many of these may reflect situations in which we are rendered powerless or are subjected to oppressive forms of power relations. In Chapter 5, I will explore how our social experiences may become internalised, thereby leaving us with particular areas of personal vulnerability – or resilience.

The relative impact of social and biological factors

Although it is often assumed that it is biological – probably genetic – factors that determine whether or not we experience mental distress, this view is not supported by the evidence. One of few study designs which has allowed the direct comparison of the relative importance of biological or social factors was Finnish research on outcomes for a large cohort of adopted children, some of whom had a close relative with a diagnosis of 'schizophrenia' (Tienari et al., 2004). Only 1.5% of those deemed to be at genetic risk but placed in supportive family settings went on to be diagnosed with 'schizophrenia' (not much more that the prevalence rate in the wider population) – as against 5% of those adoptees who were at low genetic risk, but were placed with less functional families. As we shall see, a range of other adverse social circumstances can result in prevalence rates that are up to ten times higher than that for the rest of the population. Thus, on their own, social factors would seem to have a substantially greater impact than genes – although where people may be exposed to social adversity, those with genetic susceptibility may be a substantially greater risk (ibid.).

Disadvantage, discrimination and injustice

Research has demonstrated strong correlations between the incidence of mental distress and a range of indicators of social disadvantage, including lack of education, unemployment and being brought up in poor and socially disorganised neighbourhoods, especially in inner urban areas (Fryer, 1995; Fryers et al., 2001; Rogers and Pilgrim, 2003). For example, in one study, children brought up in relatively deprived economic circumstances, but with no family history of psychosis, were found to be seven times more likely to be diagnosed with schizophrenia in later life (Harrison et al., 2001).

What is less clear from this research is the degree to which it is social deprivation itself which is damaging, or whether it is the perceived injustice of being made to feel inferior. International comparisons would suggest that there is relatively little adverse impact on mental wellbeing if one is poor within a context where everyone is poor, or within a culture where one is valued for who one is rather than what one owns. Instead, it is suggested that it is experiences of injustice, in terms of *relative* disadvantage (and the negative social connotations that may go with this), rather than *absolute* levels of deprivation, that may be more pernicious in their effects on mental health (Dohrenwend, 2000).

This fits with wider evidence to suggest that being on the 'wrong side' of any social division, where difference becomes linked with social inferiorisation and 'othering', may greatly increase vulnerability to mental distress (Janssen et al., 2003). Research findings have found that, in the UK, people from minority ethnic groups may be more likely to be diagnosed with 'schizophrenia' than White British people, with incidence being up to nine times higher for people of African Caribbean descent (Fearon et al., 2006). These differences cannot be explained by biological difference – as no significantly enhanced rates are to be found in countries of origin (Bhugra et al., 1999; Hickling and Rogers-Johnson, 1995) – or by the impact of migration, as there have been higher psychiatric admission rates among the subsequent British-born generations that those who first settled in the UK (McGovern and Cope, 1987). What is perhaps most telling is further research which suggests that, for Black people, living in a socially and economically disadvantaged (but racially mixed) inner-city area results in a lower incidence of psychiatric hospital admissions than living in a more prosperous White-dominated suburb (Boydell et al., 2001). This further reinforces the view that it is not disadvantage as such which has the greatest impact on mental health, but whether one faces discrimination or exclusion within one's everyday life (Halpern and Nazroo, 2000, p. 34) – a finding that has been confirmed by the self-reports of many Black service users (McLean et al., 2002).

Racism may impact at a number of levels. It may perhaps engender responses of anger, frustration and alienation, which may have no positive outlet if attempts to challenge racism are perceived as aggression, and lead to conflicts which rebound upon the victim. Oppression may become internalised both on an individual and on a community level (Lipsky, 1987), and its implications, in terms of taking on negatively valued or conflicted identities, are explored further in Chapter 5. It may also be reflected in social attitudes and professional practice which can 'lead to African-Caribbean people being selectively picked out and labelled as "mentally ill" where this would not be the case if they were White British' (Ferns, 2005, p. 131; see also Fernando, 2010).

Social divisions based on gender and sexual orientation may also have adverse implications on our mental health: the overall incidence of mental distress (excluding substance misuse) among women can be nearly twice as high as that among men (Prior, 1999). However, this overall statistic belies a more complex picture which suggests that a patriarchal social order (albeit one that may be changing in certain regards) may be potentially damaging to the mental health of both women and men. Gender stereotypes would seem to play a major part in this, with women who either go against the dictates of their socialisation, or are overly conforming, being at greatest risk of mental distress (Read, 2004). It is likely that the former group may face unrelenting pressure and hostility, not just from many men, but also from those women who choose to be somewhat more conforming. The latter group, while fitting in perfectly with expectations that they should always be unselfish, pleasing and deferential, may find that this is at the cost of storing up unexpressed anger and hurt inside. It is not perhaps surprising that women are more likely to experience forms of mental distress that are congruent with a deferential and powerless social role, where difficult feelings are turned inwards, as in anxiety, depression, eating disorders and self-harm.

For men, the greatest vulnerability is among those who fail to live up to the dominant constructions of masculinity: those who are 'losers' within an ethos of competition or those whose identity does not fit, perhaps due to sexual orientation, culture or ethnicity. Typically, men may tend to deal with any unease in different ways, perhaps taking it out on others, for example through criminal or anti-social behaviour, or through trying to suppress it through substance misuse, workaholism or other strategies which keep them outside formal definitions of mental distress – a repertoire of options that reflect men's relatively more dominant power positions within society. Although overall rates of incidence are similar, routes into psychosis may be different for women and men: variations in typical age of onset perhaps reflecting gender-specific stresses that may be associated with particular points within the life cycle (Read, 2004).

Although it is an area that is less well researched, there are strong indications that lesbians and gay men are significantly 'greater users of mental health services' (King et al., 2003, p. 557). The discrimination they face within wider society may lead to greater isolation and lack of social support than their heterosexual counterparts (Jorm et al., 2002). Experiences of victimisation may result in lowered self-esteem (Otis and Skinner, 1996) and a consequent internalisation of guilt and fear (Macfarlane, 1998). Unfortunately, with homosexuality still being classed as a mental disorder until the 1990s, and the past use of aversive techniques to 'correct' sexual orientations, lesbians and gay men may still experience sexuality as a taboo area in their contacts with services – leading to a lack of recognition of their needs or the provision of appropriate forms of support (Carr, 2005).

While the evidence for an association between experiences of social injustice and mental distress is strong, it has had remarkably little impact on mental health practice. Politically, it has perhaps been safer to regard mental distress as a medical condition requiring individualised treatment (even though this strategy is highly expensive), than to see elevated rates of mental distress as the consequence of social inequalities and social divisions. Nevertheless, these issues are beginning to receive greater recognition in England with the launching of mental health service strategies in relation to social exclusion (Social Exclusion Unit, 2004), women (Department of Health, 2002) and black and ethnic minorities (Department of Health, 2005) – and in the wider 'New Horizons' strategy (Department of Health, 2009).

Alongside this, there is a need for a much more rigorous look at how mental health services, and individuals' professional practice, may serve to reproduce some of the very same attitudes and practices that contribute to discrimination and injustice within the wider community (Ferns, 2005). Despite the attempts of oppressed groups to articulate their concerns and recommend changes over recent decades, relatively little has so far changed – resulting in increased cynicism, apathy and alienation, and almost certainly further contributing to levels of mental distress (Keating, 2002).

Adverse life events

Alongside the pervasive and longer-term damaging impact of oppressive social environments, there is substantial evidence that adverse life events – whether in childhood or in adult life – may increase our vulnerability to mental distress. Table 3.1 shows strong associations between lifetime exposure to certain types of 'victimising' life events and experiences of psychosis. This connects with a wider research literature which suggests that adverse life events can play a major role in rendering people vulnerable to all types of mental distress.

What is not clear from this research is the degree to which the aftermath of events such as running away from home or being looked after in local authority care may, in their own right, contribute to subsequent mental distress, or whether they simply reflect other life events such as abuse, neglect or domestic violence. While it is likely that the relative importance of different contributory factors may vary, prevalence studies indicate that care leavers remain an easily identifiable group that are up to ten times more likely than the general population to develop mental health difficulties (see also McAuley and Young, 2006).

Table 3.1 Life events and psychosis

Lifetime experience of:	Prevalence among those with 'probable psychotic disorder' (%)	Prevalence among those with 'no disorder' (%)
Sexual abuse	34.5	1.8
Being bullied	46.4	14.6
Being taken into local authority care	17.9	1.6
Violence in the home	38.1	4.1
Running away from home	34.5	2.8

Source: Selected data taken from Bebbington et al., 2004, p. 222. Reproduced with permission.

Loss and deprivation

Experiences of loss take many forms, from bereavement or enforced separation involving someone we are close to, to loss of status or lifestyle (e.g. though redundancy), loss of capacity (e.g. resulting from an accident) and loss of an anticipated future (e.g. through failure in exams). In many instances we are able to come to terms with such losses by going through a process of grieving and sadness – and it is important not to confuse such difficult (but ultimately productive) feelings with mental distress.

However, when an experience of loss interlinks with a wider context of powerlessness, dependence or isolation, we may experience it as deprivation – a sense that something precious has been forcibly taken away from us in a way that feels abusive to us. We may feel angry but have no opportunity to express this – and so the anger may be turned inwards, making it harder for us to move on from the experience. These unresolved feelings may subsequently become reflected in our ways of relating to others or in how we see ourselves. Such experiences of loss may increase vulnerability to mental distress – for example, women who lose their mothers before the age of 12 have been found to be at higher risk of depression (Brown and Harris, 1978).

Neglect

Perhaps one of the hardest experiences to define is that of neglect in childhood. It represents the absence of care, recognition and emotional responsiveness and may become reflected in our attachment style (which is discussed in more detail in Chapter 5). However, unlike events that are experienced as traumatic, neglect tends to leave no specific or vivid memories. At a practical level, children may become quite adept at nurturing themselves – so the lack may not be immediately noticeable either to the child or to others.

While there is no reliable way to measure neglect, and people may be very unclear as to whether or not their experience might constitute neglect, between one-third and two-thirds of respondents in inpatient surveys have reported experiencing physical or emotional neglect in childhood (Holowka et al., 2003; Lipshitz, 1999).

Trauma

The term 'trauma' can be somewhat overused to mean any shocking or upsetting event. I will use it in a more limited way to describe any experience that dislocates or damages our sense of self and our confidence in relating to others (see Howell, 2005). Some such experiences may be sudden and terrifying, such as rape; some may be sustained and frightening over a longer period of time, such as bullying, sexual abuse or exposure to domestic violence; while others may be disturbing in different ways – such as parental separation or the death of a close family member. What characterises most experiences of trauma is a combination of powerlessness and isolation from sources of support; and what can be particularly damaging is the impact of prolonged, repeated trauma, especially where this is characterised by subjection to totalitarian control (Herman, 1997).

It may not just be the apparent shock-value of an experience that determines how disturbing it may be to us as individuals. Our reaction may depend on:

- the invasiveness of the experience – whether it involved the violation of our personal, sexual or other boundaries;
- the degree to which we may have felt powerless to influence the course of events;
- whether it was an isolated event, or whether it was repeated and sustained;
- what the experience meant to us in terms of its impact on our key identities, relationships and attachments (e.g. whether we feel betrayed by others whom we trusted or with whom we were close);
- whether we may have been drawn into blaming ourselves (or are being blamed by others) for what happened;
- our access to supportive personal relationships;
- our personal resilience.

Fear, hurt, rage, grief and sadness are all *active* responses to extreme events and are part of coming to terms with what has happened. If we are able to work through our feelings, and have the support from others in doing so, we are less likely to be traumatised. In this way, we are able to retain our sense of personal agency: we are still in charge of our life. However, if the event and its implications are so serious, or if support is so lacking, we may find ourselves 'frozen' and unable to work through the feelings it brings up for us. Instead, we may try to repress the experience using particular defence mechanisms, which may be at some cost to our continuing personal growth and social functioning (see Chapter 5). At some point in the future, these defences may start to break down and the trauma may come back to the surface, sometimes associated with the same intensity of feeling as the original experience.

Within psychiatry, there has been a tendency to group together as 'post-traumatic stress disorder' (PTSD) the most obvious reactions to known trauma – such as flashbacks, heightened fear responses and hyper-alertness. This classification has been kept separate from mainstream psychiatric diagnoses which were not seen as trauma related. However, this separation has come to be seen as increasingly artificial, with many of the other experiences associated with PTSD, such as dissociation, hearing voices or depression, being common to other diagnoses (Hamner et al., 2000), while more in-depth exploration with many people with other diagnoses can often reveal a history of trauma and abuse, much of which may be independently substantiated (Herman and Schatzow, 1987). Given people's potential reticence in revealing painful or shameful experiences to practitioners or researchers, it is likely that traumatic experiences will tend to be underreported (especially by men, where revealing vulnerability may be problematic).

Some research has linked particular forms of trauma, such as sexual abuse, with specific manifestations of mental distress – such as self-harm or the diagnosis of 'borderline personality disorder' (Brodsky et al., 1995; Van der Kolk et al., 1991). While there may indeed be particular associations of this sort, there is strong evidence to link the aftermath of trauma with a heightened vulnerability to a wide range of mental distress experiences, including depression (Maercker et al., 2004) and psychosis (Larkin and Morrison, 2006; Read et al., 2005). Marius Romme found that a majority of those with problematic voice hearing experiences could link its onset to some specifiable trauma (Pennings and Romme, 2000), while Kilcommons and Morrison (2005) found over 90% of a sample of people with psychosis reported experiences of trauma, with a clear association between the severity of the trauma and the severity of the psychosis.

Abuse and victimisation

While most traumatic experiences involve an overall sense of powerlessness in relation to events that are beyond our control, some forms of trauma involve being *abused* by others in positions of superior power. Whether abuse is physical, emotional or sexual, its core defining characteristic is that it represents an enactment of oppressive power that exploits, violates or intrudes upon its victim – and may give the perpetrator some sense of excitement or gratification through being able to use power in this way (Plumb, 2005). Abuse may often be accompanied by the imposition of distorted rationalisations that justify the act and locate responsibility (and blame) for it with the victim (Warner, 2000). Such experiences can result in a sense of self that is marked by shame, an inability to set protective boundaries around one's body and mind, the repression and turning inwards of feelings of anger and outrage, and an inability to trust others or form secure attachments with them.

Various forms of abuse have increasingly figured in the narratives that women, and more recently men, have felt able to disclose about the circumstances that may have led to the onset of their mental distress. In an overview of research with people with psychosis, Read et al. (2005) found that on average around 70% of women and 60% of men reported child sexual or physical abuse. There can be a particular association between abuse experiences and subsequently hearing voices that are sexualised, critical and sometimes demanding of acts of self-harming behaviour. Castillo (2000) found that 88% of a sample of people with the diagnosis of 'borderline personality disorder' had a history of such abuse, 70% of whom reported being sexually abused in early childhood. However, it is important not to jump to the conclusion that *all* people who experience psychosis (or, for that matter, who self-harm or have eating disorders) are necessarily survivors of abuse. Some people have very different narratives, and it can emerge that experiences such as neglect and loss can be just as damaging as abuse.

Putting it all together

As we have seen, a broad array of adverse social experiences may increase our vulnerability to mental distress. In many instances, what seems to make a difference is not the social circumstance or life event as such, but what it means to us within the context of our identities, personalities and social relationships. Typically all such adverse experiences involve:

- powerlessness, oppression or victimisation;
- an inability to exercise personal agency;
- the enforced disruption or distortion of relationships and identities;
- the absence of social support or a safe place in which to express feelings of anger, sadness or fear.

We are just beginning to see how these factors may impact in combination. Analysis of larger population samples suggests that multiple adverse or traumatic experiences have a cumulative impact in terms of increased likelihood of breakdown (Scott et al., 2007; Shevlin et al., 2008). At an individual level, this may be seen in

M.L.'s account of the combination of experiences that led up to her breakdown (see Chapter 7, Box 7.1).

Constructive social experiences

Although the main focus of this chapter has been on damaging social experiences, we also need to consider what sorts of experiences may be constructive, in the sense of contributing to the development of our resilience (see Chapter 5). This is an area where research evidence is less clear – due to the tendency to focus on problems and deficits, rather than strengths and abilities, within much of mental health research.

To a large degree, resilience would seem to stem from what we internalise from positive experiences – of recognition, participation and connection with others, and of having opportunities to achieve and learn relevant knowledge and problem-solving capabilities. Such experiences may be easier to come by if one's background is characterised by security, affirmation and social inclusion (or, at least, an absence of 'in your face' injustice or abuse) – but more privileged social circumstances do not, on their own, guarantee resilience. Some aspects of resilience would seem only to be learned through facing more challenging experiences – and some people may develop resilience through surmounting what, on the face of it, may seem to be the very sorts of adverse experiences that others may find damaging. However, there may be subtle differences. For example, facing discrimination alone may be very different from facing the same discrimination but with support and understanding from peers or family, or with an internalised self-confidence that has been learned through other aspects of one's upbringing.

Summary of key points

- Social factors can be more important than genetics in influencing the likelihood of mental distress.
- Relative disadvantage, discrimination and injustice are major contributory factors to mental distress.
- Many experiences of mental distress can be traced back to specific experiences of trauma, abuse, loss or neglect.
- Powerlessness and isolation from sources of support are key factors in most traumatic experiences.
- Combinations of traumatic life events and adverse social circumstances can be particularly damaging.

Further reading

General:
Read, J., Mosher, L., & Bentall R. (eds) (2004). *Models of Madness.* Hove: Routledge.
Tew, J. (ed.) (2005). *Social Perspectives in Mental Health.* London: Jessica Kingsley.

Social inequalities:
Rogers, A., & Pilgrim, D. (2003) *Mental Health and Inequality.* Basingstoke: Palgrave Macmillan.

Ethnicity and culture:
Fernando, S. (2010) *Mental Health, Race and Culture* (3rd ed.). Basingstoke: Palgrave Macmillan.

Impact of trauma:
Larkin, W., & Morrison, A. (2006) *Trauma and Psychosis: New Directions for Theory and Therapy.* Hove: Routledge.

4 | Power, agency and social capital

In Chapter 3, we saw how a range of adverse social experiences may lead to an increased likelihood of experiencing mental distress. Underlying many of these are recurring themes of oppression, abuse and sheer powerlessness. In turn, most people experience mental distress as a loss of control – a loss that can be exacerbated by intrusive or controlling service responses (Campbell, 1996; Coleman, 1999a, 199b).

It is being increasingly recognised that power issues are closely implicated in the onset of mental distress. Experiences of humiliation, social defeat and entrapment are often seen as precursors of mental distress (Gilbert and Allen, 1998; Selten and Cantor-Graae, 2007). People who have come to see their relationship with the world in terms of an external locus of control – seeing their lives as being largely controlled by the actions of others – are more likely to develop psychosis in adulthood (Bentall et al., 2001; Frenkel et al., 1995). Research into voice-hearing experiences suggests that it is not so much the content of voices that can be problematic, but one's perceptions of the power relations between oneself and one's voices (Birchwood et al., 2000). In turn, these can tend to mirror how one may be situated in one's power relations with other people:

> *The more I compromise for others the more troublesome the voices become.* (Holloway, 2009, p. 217)

As we shall see in Chapter 9, empowerment and reclaiming personal efficacy are at the core of recovery from mental distress. (Chamberlin, 1997).

Particular presentations of distress may themselves refer, perhaps indirectly or metaphorically, to experiences of powerlessness or victimisation. One's thoughts may seem to be controlled by outside forces, or apparently powerful internal voices may put one down or dictate what one should or should not do. Episodes of depression or anxiety may invoke – perhaps in a more extreme way – the feelings associated with experiences of oppression or intimidation. One may symbolically revisit the power relations of abuse through acts of self-harm. Alternatively, one may escape from the actuality of powerlessness through an exaggerated belief in one's importance – for example, seeing oneself as some sort of saviour or prophet.

As we saw in Chapter 2, it is a disruption of a conventional sense of personal agency – in the sense of losing control over aspects of one's experience – that differentiates mental distress from everyday experiences of upset and difficulty. Paradoxically, some experiences of mental distress may represent desperate attempts to take control in situations where one may otherwise feel completely powerless. For example, people with eating disorders have described how they have become locked into a power struggle in which their only remaining area of control over their lives and their bodies has been to refuse (or abuse) food – thereby potentially threatening their own survival (Lawrence, 1984).

Just as loss of power and control may be central to our individual experience of mental distress, so too may be our exclusion from the social forms of power that are associated with social relationships and networks (social capital). Where we are able to access these, they may act as an important buffer against mental distress, and also provide a key component of our recovery (Nelson et al., 2001a).

In this chapter, I will develop an analysis of social power relations that can underpin mental health practice, relating this to:

- experiences of oppression or exclusion – and how we may internalise these;
- agency, personal efficacy and control over oneself and one's life;
- social capital and social connection.

However, despite the evidence that these issues may be central to many experiences of mental distress, such perspectives have been somewhat marginalised in practice. Instead, a narrower focus on individual 'pathology' has tended to frame not only biomedical approaches, but also many psychosocial approaches which may focus just on improving people's social adjustment and diminishing the impacts of their irrational drives or belief systems.

A theoretical framework for understanding and working with power relations

Within sociological and psychological theory, there is surprisingly little consensus as to how power should be understood, resulting in a lack of clarity as to how we may develop a practice that is empowering for people with mental health difficulties (Tew, 2005b). We may be all too aware of the effects of power – such as abuse – without understanding the underlying power relations which may have allowed this to happen.

Max Weber provides a rather narrow and static conception of power as 'a finite commodity to be seized or bestowed' (Masterson and Owen, 2006, p. 21). Seeing power as a 'thing' in this way can be unhelpful as it prevents us from seeing how power may be constructed in and through our social relationships. It may operate between people in ways that open up and/or close off particular personal and social opportunities. It is the prerequisite for any form of individual or collective agency (*power to*), enabling us, among other things, to:

- access, develop or control resources;
- have influence with (or over) others;
- bring about change or maintain the status quo;
- make choices or decisions;
- negotiate relationships with others;
- define our identities, or ascribe identities to others;
- protect ourselves and others from harm, abuse or exploitation (or take advantage of those who appear weaker).

Power relations may operate at a macro scale – depending on gender, race, class, age or other identities – and at more micro or localised scales in terms of the structuring of our more immediate social interactions.

One way of making sense of the complexity of power relations is to look at:

1. Is power operating in ways that are *limiting* or *productive* of opportunity?
2. Are particular social relationships characterised by the 'vertical' exercise of *power over* others, or by a more 'horizontal' development of *power together* between people through their mutual connections?

Putting these two dimensions together, we have a matrix in which each cell describes a particular way in which power may operate – enabling us to see how not all instances of *power over* are limiting, nor are all instances of *power together* productive (Tew, 2002, p. 166).

Box 4.1   Matrix of power relations

	Power Over	Power Together
Productive Modes of Power	**Protective Power** Deploying power in order to safeguard vulnerable people and enhance their opportunities	**Co-operative Power** Collective action, sharing, mutual support and challenge – through valuing commonality *and* difference
Limiting Modes of Power	**Oppressive Power** Exploiting differences to enhance own position and resources at the expense of others – or trying to resist this (if on the 'receiving end')	**Collusive Power** Banding together to exclude others or suppress awareness of different perspectives and experiences

The matrix helps to move our conception of empowering practice on from the one-dimensional perspective of a 'zero-sum' game in which one can only gain power at another's expense (Barnes & Bowl, 2001). Instead, it offers more creative and imaginative ways of generating *power to* – particularly through enabling people to mobilise *co-operative* and *protective* forms of power, and thereby shifting the balance of power relations away from *oppressive* and *collusive* forms of power.

Protective power

Feminists have highlighted how women may deploy *power over* for the benefit and protection of others – rather than for their own personal advancement (Baker Miller, 1991) – and, at a societal level, this *protective* power may also link to an 'ethic of care' (Williams, 2005). Within the context of mental health, the key to using *protective* power is to deploy it in ways that are as temporary and self-limiting as possible – providing holding and comfort for people at times of crisis or vulnerability, so as keep open the possibilities for them to reclaim control over their lives as soon as they are able.

However, there can also be a danger that *protective* power becomes *oppressive* if it is deployed in ways that are patronising or defensive: restricting rather than safeguarding the opportunities that may be open to vulnerable individuals. This can be an unfortunate feature of some instances of professional practice (Fitzsimons and Fuller, 2002). For example, actions and practices designed to safeguard vulnerable others may be experienced as intrusive or patronising – as instances of *oppressive* rather than *protective* power. The use of statutory powers to coerce can be particularly problematic (see Chapter 10); but so too can 'wrapping people in cotton wool' and preventing them from taking the personal risks that they may need to take as part of their recovery journey. This may occur particularly where agency practice and media representations may be *collusive* in constructing people either as victims of an 'illness' which will require them to be cared for and treated by others for the rest of their lives, or as inherently 'dangerous' individuals from whom the public must be protected.

Social divisions and structural forms of oppressive power

Structural oppression occurs when social differences result in a loss of 'parity of participation' – arising from systematic processes of misrecognition and subordination (Fraser and Honneth, 2003). Sometimes these processes may operate in ways that are overt and easily identifiable (as in employment discrimination), and sometimes in ways that reflect more subtle but potentially very pernicious processes of inferiorisation (through differential expectations, stereotyping and other forms of put-down). However, the domination of structural power is never total: perceived injustices may provoke opposition – and if this resistance becomes more organised, social movements may emerge that result in realignments and shifts in power relations between groups (as in the greater acceptance and equality achieved by lesbian and gay people over recent years).

As we saw in Chapter 4, people who find themselves at the 'wrong end' of social divisions tend to have a much greater likelihood of experiencing mental distress. Furthermore, not only may experiences of 'othering' contribute to mental distress; they may also be the consequence of being identified as 'mentally ill' (see Chapter 7).

Interestingly, it is not only the victims of social oppression who may experience adverse consequences to their mental health. Through their constant orientation towards achieving *power over*, dominant groups may become characterised by a ruthlessly competitive ethos and this may create its own stresses and strains for those who find it hard to reach or stay at the 'top of the pile'. Members of dominant groups who do not 'do' dominance very well, or whose identities fall outside what is expected of them, may tend to be more vulnerable to mental distress.

The localised operation of oppressive power

Alongside analyses of power in relation to wider social divisions, poststructuralists have focused on the micro-dynamics of power: how it 'comes from below', operating and being reproduced within localised situations and interpersonal interactions (Foucault, 1981, p. 94). Instead of power being seen as something which individuals may acquire in order to impose their will upon others, it is seen as already existing 'out there', as imbuing the positions and identities that may be available to people to take up within particular social discourses. Specific positions may confer relative power or power-lessness within the structuring of interactions – parents may assume power in relation to children, or professionals in relation to service users. These positionings – and their implications in terms of superiority and inferiority – may be constructed through the language we use, the places we meet in, our non-verbal signs and gestures, our patterns of greeting, the codes that govern what we can or cannot say or do, and so on. They invite us to see ourselves, and orient ourselves towards others, in particular ways that may be *oppressive* or *collusive* – or may be *co-operative* or *protective*; they may either give us *power to* or take power away from us.

For example, a situation of sexual abuse may be seen as the imposition of *oppressive* power in the absence of any effective local networks of *protective* power within family or community. Instead, the actions of the perpetrator may often be secured through the *collusion* of others turning a 'blind eye' to what may be going on or failing to be receptive to any potential cry for help from the victim. Within such a context of isolation, any attempts at resistance may be crushed or silenced by the threat of retribution.

Although there has been a tendency to see structural and poststructural analyses as opposed to one another, it is more helpful to see these as complementary. Putting the two perspectives together, we may see how structural and local forms of power relations may intersect, often in quite complex ways. Wider societal constructions of gender, 'race' or class may provide a context in which families and communities negotiate their own discourses which may redefine or resist certain elements of the dominant discourses (Fook, 2002, pp. 52–3). However, in certain situations, structural inferiorisation may intersect with and legitimate the localised imposition of *oppressive* forms of power – for example in setting the context in which women or children may be vulnerable to acts of violence or abuse.

Power and agency

The concept of agency describes our active engagement in the world around us and the manner in which we do this – in particular, how we construct ourselves as a subject, 'I', in our social interactions, and how we exert influence on the world around us, both individually and collectively. Our possibilities for agency are constrained and constructed by our social and cultural context, our location within wider systems of power relations and the capabilities and orientations towards using power that we have internalised through our past experience. As we saw in Chapter 2, experiences of mental distress tend to involve some breakdown of personal agency – with aspects of our inner experience and external circumstances taking over and driving us in ways that seem outside our executive control.

Within particular societies there can be clear prescriptions as to how one is supposed to present oneself as 'I'. In more traditional societies, ideas of subjectivity may be closely linked with ideas of duty, honour and place within family and community. In modern Western societies these tend to be predicated on a particular notion of individuality: that we are to see ourselves as free and autonomous. Although we may be encouraged to think that we are authors of our own lives, the reality of our agency as social actors may be more complex as, much of the time, we may find not just that our actions may be constrained, but also that our identities and motivations may themselves emerge from our positioning within discourses and social expectations that are not of our own making – processes of covert and latent power which may be often outside our awareness (Lukes, 2005).

Foucault takes this argument further and explores how power may be seductive: our positioning as 'I' within particular discourses and interactions may afford us opportunities for positive influence, while at the same time constraining, directing and channelling our actions and how we present ourselves to the world (1982, p. 220). This may offer us our statuses, identities and positions in relation to others, or organise us into like-minded solidarities and social groupings, but may also enforce principles of self-discipline and conformity. Thus our agency may come at a price: we 'willingly participate in practices and structures which simultaneously empower and disempower' (Fook, 2002, p. 52).

To be recognised and accepted as a citizen within modern societies, one must appear as if one is a fundamentally rational being, 'centred in a unitary, reflexive and directive consciousness', who can be held individually responsible for one's actions (DuGay et al., 2000, p. 2). However, constructing one's agency in line with this 'ideal' form of individuality may not always be straightforward as one tries to respond to contradictory demands and expectations, as well as internal conflicts or dilemmas. Nevertheless, our status will tend to be judged on how well we maintain an appearance of rationality and 'strength of character', and how reliably we hold ourselves together in order to perform our expected social roles. Any failure to deliver a sufficient appearance of coherent agency can lead to severe social sanctions – which can have particularly serious implications for people with mental distress (see Chapter 7).

Accessing and exercising power: personal efficacy

How we exercise personal agency within a given situation may depend on the degree to which we may feel comfortable and confident in using power (on our own and with others), and hence the degree to which we may feel in active control of our lives. This may be seen as the subjective aspect of empowerment – a basic confidence that we can negotiate and influence the world around us – and connects with the notion of self-efficacy that has been developed particularly within psychology (Bandura, 1977). In turn, internalising a positive sense of personal efficacy may be seen to form a key aspect of resilience (see Chapter 5).

It is important not to conceive of personal efficacy in terms of stamping our autonomous 'will' upon the world around us: as we have seen, our desires and motivations may emerge or be shaped for us through our social interactions. Nevertheless, personal efficacy comprises:

- subjective confidence that we can (and are entitled to) have an influence on our world;
- a repertoire of relevant capabilities that we can use; and
- an engagement in social relations that enables us to be 'part of the action' where power is being developed or challenged.

In practice, it may often involve linking with others in the generation and deployment of *protective* or *co-operative* power relations.

In general, we are able to develop and internalise a sense of personal efficacy if we have experience of being in situations where we can access power, where we can negotiate with others and where we have some opportunity to make a difference either to our own life or to that of others. However, not everyone may find that they are able to follow this path. Some may face social or cultural prohibitions (perhaps on the basis of gender) in relation to the assertive use of power, and may therefore have to rely on more indirect and potentially fragile strategies for influence. Those who have been consistently subject to the oppressive power of others may have developed little inbuilt confidence in handling power to their advantage and have come to accept that the course of their lives will continue to be determined by the actions and expectations of powerful others (an assumed external locus of control).

Victimisation, 'failed struggle' and the internalisation of oppression

Victimisation involves direct experience of oppression, abuse or deprivation, coupled with a wider context of *collusive* power which traps us within a situation and denies us access to protection or support. If our attempts at resistance are met with superior power and overruled, we may reach the point of 'failed struggle' (Gilbert, 1992). Instead of anger becoming an energising force for mobilising action or resistance, it may have to be held inside as an unresolved sense of rage or hurt.

In order to survive the situation, we may need to invoke a range of strategies to defend ourselves against the worst of what is happening, and in order to contain our internal 'hot potato' of unexpressed rage or hurt. These may involve being 'devious' or 'manipulative' in order to protect ourselves or have some influence over our situation. In more extreme situations where influence may be impossible, we may simply give up and turn everything inwards. Either way, enacting these strategies may be at some personal cost to our sense of self and ways of relating to others, and may involve developing internal defence mechanisms that can constrain and impair our ability to function in the world (see Chapter 5).

As a result of such processes of humiliation and entrapment, being on the 'wrong' end of *oppressive* and *collusive* power relationships may come to be internalised as self-limiting or self-destructive attitudes, feelings or patterns of behaviour. These may embody and re-enact our experience of oppression and can, in turn, make us vulnerable to mental distress. In a study of the life events that predisposed women to depression (Brown et al., 1995), experiences of humiliation figured strongly, often resulting from events such as verbal, physical or sexual assaults which may have undermined their ability to construct any positive sense of self.

Social capital: co-operative or collusive power?

Our informal social networks of friendship and acquaintance, together with our more formal connections (perhaps through our work), can open up a range of social opportunities – from mutual support and practical assistance to developing interests and advancing our aspirations. Though analogy with economic capital, this is termed social capital, the 'features of social life – networks, norms and trust – that enable participants to act together more effectively to pursue shared objectives' (Puttnam, 1996, p. 56). Unfortunately, Puttnam's communitarian vision situates social capital as a universal good that benefits all – and fails to take into account social divisions and power relations within societies. However, Bourdieu offers a more grounded conception of social capital as a networks of *power together* in which people may be included or have access – but where those already 'in' may use more or less explicit 'conservation strategies' in order to keep out those who are considered less desirable (1977).

At a theoretical level, it has been concepts of social capital that have provided the tools by which to analyse barriers to, and enablers of, social inclusion. It is seen as comprising two distinct aspects which interconnect with one another:

- *Structural social capital*: the infrastructure of friendships, family relationships, social networks, meeting places and activities that enable people to connect with one another on a formal or informal basis and where social 'business' is transacted. In turn, this is governed and enabled by shared norms, such as mutual trust, reciprocity or sense of community – and also by rules that determine who may have access or be included.
- *Cognitive social capital*: people's attitudes, beliefs and knowledge of 'the right way to do things' that may enable them to engage with the various networks and opportunities that may exist within communities.

We can only develop our cognitive social capital through being allowed (at least limited) access to structural social capital, and we need a modicum of cognitive social capital if we are to access most forms of structural social capital.

It can also be helpful to distinguish between two types of social capital which offer different approaches to *power together*:

- *Bonding* social capital concerns strong ties of mutual connection, typically constructed around a shared identity of 'people like us'. Bonding social capital may provide people with a key to mutual support, respect and a sense of belonging or solidarity (particularly in the face of adversity or discrimination). These may be seen as instances of *co-operative power*. However, people may also use bonding social capital in a way that is *collusive* – creating a shared identity that excludes those who are not seen to fit in.

- *Bridging* social capital involves establishing connections across social and identity divisions, potentially to mutual benefit. It may involve weaker but more strategic ties that enable access to wider resources and opportunities – an approach to *co-operative power* that tends to characterise the orientation of the upwardly mobile middle classes. It may also provide opportunities for those in relatively powerless positions through forming alliances with people who may be in very different positions of structural power – for example, service users and carers working together with professionals to pursue shared objectives.

Our ability to access both *bonding* and *bridging* aspects of social capital may play a crucial role in helping us to deal with problems of living that might otherwise tip us over into mental breakdown, and in supporting our recovery if we have come to experience mental distress.

If we are to explore the realities of social life for people with mental distress, we need to move beyond seeing social capital as a general 'good' that benefits the whole community. Instead, we may need to employ a more critical approach that can distinguish between *co-operative* and *collusive* forms of *power together*, and can locate this within an understanding of divisions within communities. The finding that Black people may actually fare worse, in terms of their mental health, in white-dominated areas with high overall indices of social capital suggests that the benefits of social capital do not necessarily flow out to all sections of society (Boydell et al., 2001). It would seem that being stuck on the outside of a close-knit and mutually supportive community, and being on the wrong end of their *collusive* 'conservation strategies', may be particularly damaging for one's mental health.

Once labelled as 'mental' in some way, people may find that they rapidly lose much of their access to *bonding* and *bridging* social capital (see Chapter 7). Recovery may involve reclaiming some of this, and also establishing new forms of *bonding* social capital (perhaps through peer support with others) and new forms of *bridging* social capital that enable them to break out of the mental health 'ghetto' and access wider social opportunities.

Supportive relationships

While social capital provides an infrastructure of potential contacts and resources, and internalised orientations and capabilities which may enable us to access these, the key to social support is what this may actually deliver for in terms of personal relationships that are reliable and affirmative. As well as enhancing our general mental wellbeing, effective social support and confiding personal relationships may reduce the likelihood of problems of living turning into mental distress – and such relationships have also been identified as central to the process of recovery (see Chapter 9).

In the long term, what may be most important are relationships that are mutual, allowing one to give as well as take and to embrace differences as well as commonalities. The most effective relationships, in terms of generating *co-operative* power, are those that provide both affirmation and challenge to each participant. In this way, they may create opportunities for learning, enjoyment and development, and enable one to take up social opportunities that one might not have been able to access on one's own. Whether they are more intimate partner or family relationships, or less intense relationships with friends and colleagues, the key characteristic of a supportive relationship is one that combines mutuality with an implicit entitlement to help in times of need, without any immediate expectation of reciprocation (*protective* power). Unfortunately, the potential value of close relationships may sometimes be compromised by tensions or difficulties within them and people may need help in resolving these (see Chapter 6). Alongside this, what can be particularly valuable for people with mental distress is to develop peer support with others who have similar experiences and can offer a particular kind of understanding and mutuality (Clay et al., 2005; see also Chapter 9).

Summary of key points

- Processes of empowerment are central to mental health practice and enabling recovery.
- Power is constituted within our social relationships.
- Power relations may be *co-operative, protective, oppressive* or *collusive*.
- Mental distress is characterised by the breakdown of a coherent sense of agency (no longer appearing to be in control of oneself).
- Positive experiences of using power can be internalised as personal efficacy.
- Experiences of oppression may be internalised and reproduced in ways that make us vulnerable to mental distress.
- Empowerment and mental wellbeing may depend on accessing *bonding* and *bridging* forms of social capital.
- Social support depends on having affirmative and confiding relationships which may entitle one to help in times of need.

Further reading

Theories of power in relation to practice:
Dominelli, L. (2002) *Anti-Oppressive Social Work Theory and Practice.* Basingstoke: Palgrave Macmillan.
Tew, J. (2002) *Social Theory, Power and Practice.* Basingstoke: Palgrave Macmillan
Thompson, N. (2006) *Power and Empowerment.* Lyme Regis: Russell House.

Theories of social capital:
Halpern, D. (2004) *Social Capital.* Cambridge: Polity Press.

5 | Personality adaptations, resilience and vulnerability

In Chapters 3 and 4, we have seen how a range of adverse life events and subjection to oppressive or collusive forms of power may lead to increased likelihood of mental health difficulties. However, not everyone who is exposed to potentially damaging social experiences goes on to experience mental distress.

In this chapter, we will explore the next piece of the jigsaw: how our personality adaptations and coping strategies may provide the 'missing link' between problematic social experiences and mental distress. It is these that may determine whether we are able to deal with challenging or stressful situations (resilience) or whether we become trapped in patterns of thinking, feeling or acting that may ultimately tip us over into mental distress (vulnerability).

From 'personality disorders' to personality adaptations

The concept of 'personality disorder' can be particularly unhelpful in suggesting a permanent (and potentially untreatable) flaw in personality that is divorced from any context whereby it could be seen as meaningful response rather than mere aberration. However, this conceptualisation bears little resemblance to reality. People's difficulties tend to relate to particular situations; they are not continuous – and it may therefore be more helpful to conceive of personality issues in terms of underlying vulnerabilities (Tyrer, 2007). Furthermore, the orientations of our personalities do change over time, particularly in response to our current social environment – and people, even with more extreme diagnoses such as 'borderline personality disorder', have a tendency to find more comfortable ways of accommodating to the world as they grow older (Cohen et al., 1994). Finally, we are becoming increasingly aware that personality issues are likely to be responses to difficult, abusive or traumatic social circumstances, particularly in childhood (Brodsky et al., 1995; Castillo, 2000).

Through the practice of differential diagnosis, personality issues are conventionally divorced from any understanding of more 'acute' experiences of mental distress: one is either 'mentally ill' or 'personality disordered'. However, research findings show that the majority of people who are diagnosed with mental 'illness' may also fit the criteria for 'personality disorder' (Keown et al., 2002), suggesting that it can be the very same personality issues that attract the label of 'disorder' that can make us vulnerable to episodes of mental distress.

Therefore, instead of 'personality disorder', I will develop the less pejorative concepts of *personality adaptation* and *coping strategy* – which involve patterns of thinking, feeling and behaviour that are made in response to particular social circumstances. They may be functional for us within certain social contexts – and thereby contribute to our resilience – or may leave us vulnerable to particular forms of social stresses. Paradoxically, the very adaptations or strategies that may have been crucial in ensuring survival in difficult circumstances in childhood may turn out to be less than helpful in navigating through the very different life situations that we may encounter in adult life. Especially when taken to extremes, they may become problematic in their own right *and* they can also render us vulnerable to developing more acute forms of mental distress when we may find ourselves unable to deal with particular problems of living.

Our adaptations may be reinforced through our interaction with our social environment – vicious circles of damaging social experiences feeding into dysfunctional adaptations (and vice versa), or virtuous circles of positive social experiences helping to enhance our resilience. However, such continuities may be relatively fragile and new social circumstances may challenge and destabilise our existing adaptations and coping strategies – for good or ill.

Resilience

Within mental health services, there has been a tendency to focus on people's problems and 'illnesses' at the expense of exploring their resilience and coping abilities. However, any practice that is oriented towards recovery and wellbeing must focus at least as much on people's strengths (Saleebey, 2006). We therefore need to develop a clearer understanding of the mechanisms of resilience: what is it in our personalities and our ways of interacting that enable us to deal more effectively with stressful or upsetting situations?

Resilience involves the internalisation and re-enactment of positive experiences of *empowerment, affirmation, achievement* and *connection*. Its capabilities and orientations can be acquired and maintained through active processes of social engagement, challenge and overcoming difficulty (Stevenson and Zimmerman, 2005) – but within contexts of *protective* and *co-operative* power that contain risks and provide opportunities for connection and recognition.

It may be harder to develop resilience if one is subject to systematic forms of discrimination or inferiorisation – although having access to other situations where there may be support or protection may provide some compensation. Interestingly, experiences of privilege or dominance are not necessarily good for resilience either, as they may also isolate people from opportunities for co-operation and connection. The epidemiological evidence shows that, although those at the top end of more divided societies fare better in terms of their mental health than those at the bottom end, they still fare worse than those who are part of more connected and socially just societies (Wilkinson, 2005).

Vulnerability

Experiences of mental distress tend not to come 'out of the blue' (although it may seem this way at the time) but may reflect particular vulnerabilities which may adversely affect our ability to deal with certain forms of stress or problems of living (Zubin and Spring, 1977). Vulnerability is rarely global – most people have areas of strength and resilience, but also particular sensitivities or trigger points.

While there may be a significant genetic component in this, much of our vulnerability can stem from adverse social experiences and relationship difficulties, especially in childhood. Experiences of oppression, loss and failed struggle may be internalised and reproduced through a range of cognitive, emotional and behavioural adaptations that may subsequently make us vulnerable to mental distress. Such patterns of response and ways of perceiving ourselves and others may limit our ability to engage constructively with those around us; and the ways in which we try to contain painful or conflictual experiences may be at the expense of being able to get on with our lives and resolve current difficulties.

Interactions between the social and the biological

Although it is beyond the scope of this chapter, we must be aware of the complex interrelationship between the physiological and the psychosocial. On the one hand, genetic and other biological factors may play a part in setting the template for the ongoing development of our personalities. On the other, brain scanning research is demonstrating the degree to which the impact of social experiences may also become embedded as part of our physiology in our hormone levels and in the hard-wiring of the neural connections in our brains (Shonkoff and Phillips, 2000). Subsequent social or therapeutic experiences that are more positive may, over time, be reflected in a gradual process of physiological readaptation (Goldapple et al., 2004; Roffman et al., 2005). Thus, someone whose early life was dominated by interactions with chaotic or abusive adults may not develop the neural pathways by which to 'do' trust. However, subsequent experiences of support, consistency and protection may start to stimulate dormant pathways into activity, and practising new ways of experiencing self and others may trigger parallel processes of physiological change. In this way, the capability to trust may become established.

This can be a particularly helpful perspective in understanding the pace at which people with entrenched mental health difficulties may be able to change: brief therapy may not always be realistic if people need to reconstruct aspects of the hard-wiring of their brains.

Dynamics of social and family relationships

We do not develop our particular personality adaptations and coping strategies in isolation: we always do this within the context of the particular family and social relationships of which we are part. The two may be mutually influential – our particular adaptations and orientations may impact on our relationships and vice versa. This reciprocal interaction can be mutually enhancing where it develops out of constructive social experiences, but it can also become more of a vicious circle if it is in response to experiences such as trauma. An individual may perhaps react by becoming withdrawn, aggressive or losing their self-esteem, and this may then lock into wider relationship dynamics dominated by guilt, blame or recrimination, resulting in increasing alienation, loss of support or stigmatisation (see Chapter 6).

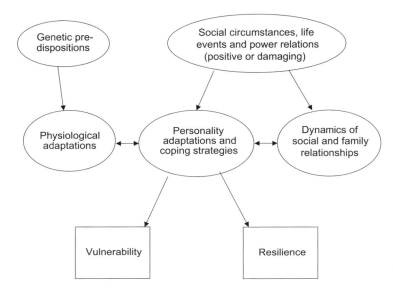

Figure 5.1 The construction of resilience and vulnerability

Social experiences and personality adaptations: towards a model of resilience and vulnerability

From the forgoing discussion, we may see how social experiences may shape our personality adaptations and coping strategies. This suggests a more comprehensive model in which our personality, our brain physiology and our modes of social participation all evolve in parallel with one another through processes of mutual interaction, influenced to some extent by genetic predispositions and, more importantly, by how our responses to particular constructive or damaging social experiences may become internalised as part of our ways of dealing with our social world. In turn, these may either promote greater vulnerability or resilience (see Figure 5.1).

Specific adaptations: implications for resilience and vulnerability

A number of themes are emerging from research as to the sorts of personality adaptations and coping styles that can contribute to resilience (Lexmond and Reeves, 2009; Moran and Eckenrode, 1992; Reivich and Shatté, 2002; Rutter, 1990). Each of these may be seen to represent one end of a continuum where, at the opposite end, are adaptations that may cause vulnerability (see Table 5.1). Each will be discussed in more detail in the subsequent sections.

Table 5.1 Adaptations, resilience and vulnerability

Area of adaptation	Adaptations that promote resilience	Adaptations that create vulnerability
Orientation towards power	Personal efficacy – confidence and capabilities	Learned helplessness, (re)victimisation or turning power against oneself
Sense of self and social identities	Self-esteem and affirmative social identities	Fragile, negative or conflicting self-identities
Ways of relating	Secure attachment style; cognitive social capital	Insecure or avoidant attachment style; alienated social disposition
Cognition and emotionality	Emotional intelligence and cognitive capability	Distorted appraisal of current experiences; limited ability to manage thoughts and feelings
Coping style	Active coping style and broad repertoire of coping strategies	Defence mechanisms or response patterns that may impair functioning

Orientations towards power: personal efficacy or re-enactment of powerlessness

In Chapter 4, we saw how facing life's challenges within a context of *co-operative* and *protective* power relations can enable us to develop and internalise a positive sense of personal efficacy and practical capabilities in developing and using *power to*. This may be cemented in beliefs and narratives that construct us as active, effective and able to respond to challenging situations. Research suggests that the people who are most resilient under stress are those who perceive themselves as capable of having influence and so adopt an active coping style when faced with adversity (Kobasa, 1979; Mancini and Bonamo, 2006). Such an orientation connects with the notion of 'learned optimism' (as opposed to 'learned helplessness') – patterns of thinking and emotional orientation that are underpinned by an outlook on life which assumes that positive outcomes may be achievable (Seligman, 1991).

However, if one's experience of power has been a longer-term pattern of failed struggle, and one has no countervailing sources of *protective* or *co-operative* power, one may come to internalise an 'involuntary subordinate self-perception' (Gilbert, 1992), abandoning the idea that one could have efficacy and operating on the basis of an assumed external locus of control. This may lead to alternative forms of adaptation, including:

- repeatedly falling into scenarios of victimisation – where the power relations and 'rules of the game' are at least familiar if unpleasant;
- passivity and learned helplessness (Seligman, 1974) – almost giving up on the idea of agency altogether. This may often be accompanied by a sense of hopelessness and lack of motivation;
- directing one's agency against oneself – perhaps by self-harming;
- desperately trying to retain some vestige of control over one's life, albeit in ways that may be self-damaging – such as becoming obsessional or anorexic.

Such orientations may begin to undermine any conventional construction of personal agency or one's ability to make supportive or empowering relationships. They may be underpinned by acquired beliefs and attributions about oneself that are self-limiting or self-destructive. If such orientations escalate, they may start to be reflected in specific experiences of mental distress.

Sense of self and performance of identity

In our interaction with our social world we perform a range of social identities that reflect our positioning within social and cultural discourses and interlink with our reflective sense of who we are. Two themes can be particularly important in determining how these identities may impact on our resilience or vulnerability:

1. Do they provide us with recognition and esteem?
2. Do they give us a sense of personal coherence or are they characterised by internal conflict?

Our identities and self-representations reflect our connections and relationships with others (Hollway, 2009; Surrey, 1985) – as well as our repudiation of what we may construct as 'other', such as defining our sexuality on the basis that we are 'not gay'. In this, we may be influenced both by our social contexts and our own ways of 'storying' who we are in response to our social experiences (Hermans, 2003; Somers, 1994). Some aspects of identity are collective and link to already existing systems of social signification, such as gender, 'race' or sexual orientation (Hall, 2000), while others are constructed as part of our positioning within family, work or other social systems. Within prevailing power relations, certain identities may accord us positive recognition, while others may set us apart as 'other' and inferior. For example, despite collective struggles to reclaim affirmative Black identities, many Black people may find that they are still playing out aspects of identity in which, at some level, they feel they have to apologise for their non-Whiteness in their interactions with White people (Fanon, 1967). Similarly, at a more local scale, other forms of perceived difference may become labelled as deviant, giving people identities that are seen as 'spoiled' in some way (Goffman, 1963).

Despite the complexity and potential conflict inherent in constructions of self and identity (Elliot, 2007), some people identify a relatively coherent 'core' sense of self that may help them through challenging situations or provide them with something around which to organise their recovery:

> I have always felt in the darkest times that there is a me inside that I can draw upon … There is inside of me a self [that] includes, but is greater than, my chemicals, my background and my traumas. It is the me that I am seeking to become in my relationships in that moment of creative uncertainty when I make contact with another.
> (Fisher, 1994, p. 2)

Past and present experience of being able to access positively valued identities can become internalised as a sense of self-esteem – one that may be relatively durable even during periods of adversity or difficulty, and thereby provide a crucial component of resilience.

However, not everyone is able to construct or hold on to such a sense of self – and this may make them more vulnerable to mental distress or their recovery more difficult. The consequences of acquiring stigmatised or subordinated identities can be very powerful: they are likely to set us on a path where, whatever we do, we may just be seen only in relation to these identities – leading us to internalise a negative self-image and a fragile sense of self.

Many experiences of mental distress involve crises of identity, and those who find their identities consistently misrecognised or denigrated within dominant social relations tend to be more vulnerable. At an individual level, Pennings and Romme note how the distressing psychotic experiences of a young gay man seemed to result from his family refusing to accept his identity once he had 'come out' (2000, p. 55). However, for some lesbian and gay people, compensatory affirmation may come through participation in subcultural lifestyles which can contribute 'to the development of a self in which one's sexuality is valued' (Moon, 1996, p. 90).

As we have seen, there is a heightened incidence of mental distress among African Caribbean people in the UK and, while the incidence of distress was high for the generation who had to renegotiate their identities on arrival in a somewhat hostile Britain, it has been even higher among those born in Britain who may find it particularly hard to build stable and affirmative identities within a context of ongoing racism and the contradictions of being 'Black' and 'British' (Frederick, 1991).

More generally, those who have to live up to the expectations of powerful others may find serious discrepancies between internalised images of how they 'ought' to be and how they actually see themselves – which may become a source of vulnerability (Higgins, 1987). At a more extreme level, enduring experiences such as sexual abuse can violate one's sense of self, leaving a sense of hollowness where one's self is no longer linked to one's own desiring and emotionality – and may feel 'spoiled' or 'dirty'.

Feeling split between conflicting and devalued identities may render us more vulnerable to mental distress – barely able to hold things together at the best of times and easily knocked off balance by the emergence of new demands or expectations. Similarly, achieving social recognition on the basis of identities that are at odds with our desires and aspirations can be at some personal cost – the affirmation that comes with having 'to live a lie' can be a very fragile way of sustaining oneself:

> *When I left home ... I knew how to act so that people would like me ... But the problem was that this role excluded so many other sides of me. I went around feeling like I was playing a role in relation to other people and I got really scared that they would see through me, see who I really was and how dumb I was and how scared I was ...* ('M', quoted in Topor et al., n.d., pp. 5–6)

Attachment styles and personal boundaries

Key factors in contributing to our resilience or vulnerability are the ways in which we go about making (or avoiding) relationships with others. Attachment theory offers a way of conceptualising 'the propensity of human beings to make strong affectional bonds to particular others' and, if things go wrong, of 'explaining ... many forms of emotional distress and personality disturbance' (Bowlby, 1982, p. 39). It is suggested that children may adopt different attachment 'styles', depending on the responses they receive from significant others (Ainsworth et al., 1978).

A key source of resilience is a *secure* attachment style which arises out of childhood (and adult) experiences that key people will be around for us on an ongoing basis – that if they go they can be trusted to return, and that others will be around for us in the meantime. (Bowlby's overemphasis on the role of full-time mothers can be unhelpful, as over-reliance on one individual may be a somewhat fragile arrangement). This internalised mindset can provide the foundation for us to approach interpersonal relationships without great anxiety and with a repertoire of skills in managing relationships, including the not-so-good bits such as dealing with conflict.

Vulnerability to subsequent mental distress may arise through the re-enactment of *avoidant* or *insecure* attachment styles. These may be adopted if no caregiver has shown any consistent interest or desire to connect with us, if there was abuse, abandonment or loss, or if a significant other became over-involved, seeking to meet their own needs or deal with their own insecurities through their relationship with us. An *avoidant* attachment style may be underpinned by deeply held negative beliefs about the value of others and lead to an underdeveloped ability to make close relationships – but may also involve sophisticated strategies for self-nurturing, such as the creation of a well-developed inner world of fantasy and helpful dialogues with internal voices. An *insecure* attachment style is characterised by anxiety in relation to feared loss (perhaps clinging on to relationships with others who may have become disinterested or even abusive), or eruptions of anger in relation to perceived rejection (past and current). At its more extreme, such inconsistency or volatility, especially when combined with a fragile sense of self, may lead to the diagnostic label of 'borderline personality disorder'.

Closely linked to the idea of attachment is that of personal boundaries: secure attachments involve having ways of negotiating personal space as well as closeness, and having lives that are separate as well as interconnecting. Experiences of abuse involve infringement of our physical and emotional boundaries – with a powerful other intruding into some of our private or intimate space without our permission or control (Plumb, 2005). This can leave a legacy of difficulties around recognising, setting and negotiating our interpersonal boundaries – we may either withdraw into a large protective 'bubble' for fear of further infringement, or, craving closeness, we may fail to set any boundaries, leading to unguarded intimacy with its potential for further abuse or feeling overwhelmed by the other. Both of these tendencies compromise our ability to sustain supportive personal relationships – and hence may contribute to our vulnerability.

Social dispositions and cognitive social capital

Alongside our more immediate personal attachments, we may develop more general orientations towards social engagement – our social 'disposition' (Bourdieu, 1990). This links with the idea of cognitive social capital: our beliefs, confidence and capabilities that enable us to reach out to wider networks of acquaintance and social opportunity. Our disposition influences how we appraise others and may determine whether we approach particular social interactions with confidence (or even assumed dominance), or whether we carry with us a message of inferiority or undeservingness. In turn, it is our enactment of our disposition that can determine how we are perceived by the gatekeepers of social networks and resources, and whether we are seen as 'the right sort of person' to be permitted access.

Cognitive social capital involves a basic belief that social connections can be worthwhile and an ability to trust (and to determine who may be trustworthy) – and it also requires a knowledge of the 'rules of the game' within particular social and cultural contexts. It is most readily developed within contexts where social support is available – through family, peer or other social networks (Pinkerton and Dolan, 2007) – and can be an important contributor to resilience, enabling one to access bonding or bridging forms of social capital and the social opportunities and safety nets that this can provide.

However, being brought up within contexts of social deprivation or exclusion can mean that one has not acquired the codes or confidence that would allow the establishment of many social connections – except perhaps within a somewhat limiting and inward looking subculture of bonding social capital within a marginalised social grouping. Particular adverse social experiences, such as trauma or abuse, may lead people to lose trust of others in a general sense – and any confidence in their ability to negotiate social relationships and to read social situations correctly. Such social experiences may lead to the development of a more alienated social disposition, perhaps involving a tendency to isolate oneself, or to engage in social interactions with a degree of wariness, ambivalence or outright hostility that may stand in the way of accessing forms of *co-operative* power or social support.

Cognitive and emotional capability

Though the current organisation of our personalities, we are continually negotiating our desires and aspirations with the expectations and opportunities presented by our social world. This process may not be straightforward, as our desires and aspirations may be complex and contradictory. What can make this process of negotiation more or less successful are our cognitive and emotional capabilities.

Cognitive capabilities involve our development of 'thinking styles' that are flexible, help us to check out and make sense of what is going on for us (both internally and externally) and are geared towards active engagement and problem solving. Cognitive theorists have shown how much of our perception, thinking and decision making is influenced by a schema of basic beliefs that we hold about ourselves, other people and our social world (Beck et al., 1979). These beliefs are grounded in our prior social experience (particularly in childhood) and may or may not be very appropriate for guiding us through the very different demands and situations that we may encounter in adult life.

Emotional capabilities (or 'emotional intelligence') involve our capacity to be in touch with and express our feelings, be sensitive to the feelings of others, and to regulate our emotional experience and expression (Goleman, 1995; Salovey et al., 1999). Again such capabilities are influenced by our prior and current social experiences, including our socialisation on the basis of culture and gender. Women may learn to inhibit expression (or even awareness) of anger (Baker Miller, 1991). They may tend to do most of the emotional 'work' involved in maintaining relationships (Duncombe and Marsden, 1993) – often by becoming particularly sensitive to the needs and emotions of others at the expense of asserting (or even being aware of) their own. By contrast, men may be encouraged to suppress not only 'weak' emotions, such as fear or sadness, but also empathy or sensitivity towards the feelings of others – so that needs and desires may become transmuted into demands, and the only emotion that can easily be expressed is anger (Kilmartin, 2005). While such constructions of emotionality may suit the performance of dominance, the resulting emotional illiteracy may have a serious downside in terms of creating vulnerability when things are not going well (Featherstone et al., 2007).

The cognitive and the emotional are closely interconnected in our appraisal of ourselves and of external situations (Ellis, 2001) – and the development of our capabilities are strongly influenced by our exposure to constructive or damaging social situations and how we have responded to these. Environments that are both affirming and challenging are likely to foster the acquisition of thinking and emotional styles that are flexible and attuned to the accurate appraisal of current situations and possibilities for positive social engagement.

However, if one is forced to subordinate oneself to the expectations of others, or is subject to systematic forms of abuse, one may develop a cognitive style that is dominated by self-limiting or self-destructive thoughts that may undermine self-esteem and may even justify one's inferiorisation. Alongside this, one may become disconnected from one's own desires and feelings and perhaps substitute a 'fog' of generalised anxiety or depression – which may actually represent a turning inwards of feelings of rage, hurt, fear or sadness.

Coping strategies, response patterns and defence mechanisms

The most immediate test of how we may deal with stresses and problems of living is in our repertoire of coping strategies, response patterns and defence mechanisms. Resilience depends on being able to access a broad repertoire of coping strategies which enable us to engage actively with whatever challenges we may face. Such active coping styles are facilitated by our personal efficacy, positive self-identities, secure attachment styles, engaged social dispositions and cognitive and emotional capabilities. Where these factors may be absent, or are insufficient when faced with particular challenges, we may have recourse to a range of response patterns and defence mechanisms, which may have become embedded within our personalities and may subsequently be triggered when we face difficult and stressful situations. Some of these may be functional for us (at least in certain circumstances) but some may be increasingly desperate and be at considerable cost to our wellbeing.

As children, when we may have found ourselves in situations of failure and powerlessness, we may develop patterns of cognitive and emotional response based on our best interpretation of what we had to do in order to 'get things right' and deal with the expectations or actions of powerful others (Kahler, 1974). For example, we may decide that we will get through if we manage not to make any 'mistakes' – so our coping strategy becomes one of perfectionism. While this may indeed be helpful in dealing with some situations, it may, if taken too far, tip into a response pattern of obsessionality that becomes a problem in itself.

Other response patterns may be driven by core beliefs about other people. For example, someone may learn, through difficult life experiences, to be cautious of others' intentions and to be vigilant in relation to possible threats. Such caution and vigilance may be very appropriate coping strategies in some situations. However, if this becomes embedded as a more generalised adaptation, it may escalate into a more general suspiciousness or paranoid outlook – which may interfere with everyday social interaction and result in greater personal vulnerability.

Faced with experiences that seem too painful or terrifying to deal with in the here-and-now, we may go further and employ a range of *defence mechanisms* – strategies and adaptations that may help to contain internal tensions or the impact of difficult experiences, and keep these out of awareness (Freud, 1968). Whereas resolving an issue involves awareness of different aspects of the experience (both good and bad), defence mechanisms insulate us from the intensity of what we cannot bear to face – perhaps relating to potentially traumatic situations such as loss or abuse.

Some defences may be active and (to some extent) intentional. They may include using drugs or alcohol to try to blot out painful memories or feelings, or using self-harming behaviours to cover over a deeper hurt or hollowness inside. Others strategies may be more unconscious, involving processes such as denial, dissociation, or projection onto others of elements of experiences that seem unacceptable – as in some psychotic or voice-hearing experiences.

While defence mechanisms may have once represented our best available survival strategy, they may be at some considerable cost in terms of our ability to function in the here-and-now, making us more vulnerable to breaking down in the face of current problems of living. Furthermore, such mechanisms may be somewhat fragile, and parts of the repressed experience may erupt back into our current awareness and threaten to take us over – perhaps in somewhat of a disguised form as persecutory voices or as the driver for uncontrollable mood swings.

Personality adaptations, coping strategies and lifestyle issues

This chapter has started to provide a bridge between sociological and psychological understandings of how we function, and thereby explore mechanisms whereby social experiences become translated into specific adaptations. However, the interrelationships between inner worlds and external functioning can be reciprocal. The particular adaptations that we make in how we deal with our world have direct implications in terms of the sort of lifestyle that we may lead. Our personal efficacy will determine whether we take the initiative or tend to fit in passively with whatever we are given. Our identities and attachment styles can lead us to seek out (or fall into) relationships that fit with our familiar patterns and expectations. Our social disposition will influence whether we engage in an active social life or become socially isolated. And specific coping strategies or defence mechanisms – such as self-harming or using drugs or alcohol – may impact greatly on our lifestyle and social relationships.

In general, adaptations and lifestyles are likely to influence one another in ways that can be mutually reinforcing. Our adaptations that may confer resilience may lead us into lifestyle choices and social relationships that, in turn, provide opportunities for us to develop our resilience. Conversely, problematic adaptations are likely to feed into problematic lifestyles that may, for example, re-create the all-too-familiar dynamics of victimhood.

However, such patterns may sometimes be challenged by current situations or relationships that do not fit with what has been experienced before. Those with a secure attachment style or engaged social disposition may find this disrupted (temporarily or more permanently) if they are faced with a traumatic loss or separation in later life – and this may also impact on their sense of self and personal efficacy. On the other hand, people with insecure attachment styles and little cognitive social capital may settle down and become more integrated, if they are able to enter into more stable adult relationships in their social or personal life.

In this way, we may see the degree to which the personal (and the specific vulnerabilities and resiliences that go with this) is socially constructed – but, at the same time, how our social world (and the stresses and supports that go with this) can be strongly influenced by our personal orientations. It is only by having theoretical frameworks that enable us to explore this that we may be able to make sense of the complex pathways that may lead some of us into experiences of mental distress.

Summary of key points

- Personality adaptations and coping styles can endow us with resilience *or* vulnerability.
- Adaptations are made in response to social experiences:
    - vulnerability reflects internalised oppression and deprivation;
    - resilience is developed through accessing productive forms of power.

- Specific adaptations involve our
  - orientations towards power and personal efficacy;
  - sense of self and social identities;
  - ways of relating;
  - cognition and emotionality;
  - coping styles, patterns of response and defence mechanisms.
- 'Personality disorders' are best understood as adaptations made under difficult circumstances – which may change in response to more positive social experiences.
- Our adaptations may influence, and be influenced by, our lifestyles.

Further reading

Cramer, P. (2006) *Protecting the Self; Defense Mechanisms in Action.* New York: Guilford Press.

Elliot, A., & DuGay, P. (2009) *Identity in Question.* London: Sage.

Goleman, D. (1995) *Emotional Intelligence.* New York: Bantam.

Harre, R. (1998) *The Singular Self: An Introduction to the Psychology of Personhood.* London: Sage.

Sanders, D., & Wills, F. (2005) *Cognitive Therapy.* London: Sage.

Snyder, C., & Lopez S. (2006) *Positive Psychology.* London: Sage.

6 | Families, relationships and social systems

Within our understanding of mental distress, and in the organisation of service responses to it, there can be an unhelpful tendency to individualise issues, with a primary focus on the internal mental 'pathology' of one person and, perhaps also, the needs of a single identified 'carer'. Typically, both of these people inhabit wider social contexts of family, friends, work colleagues, faith communities, and so on – and their sense of wellbeing or distress may be intimately interconnected with what is going on in their various social relationships. Many of their difficulties, and the potential solutions to those difficulties, are to be found by looking 'outside the box' of individualisation.

In this chapter, I will explore how families and interpersonal relationships may, on the one hand, provide vital support in dealing with unease or distress, while, on the other, may themselves have become carriers of tension and discord. I will review research findings in relation to the impact of family and relationship dynamics upon mental health, and explore the potential contribution of systems theory in providing the tools whereby we can explore relationships and patterns of social interaction.

Families and caring

Over recent years, policy and legislative discourses have tended to construct separate and individualised categories of 'service user' and 'carer', with particular sets of assumptions defining both their relationship to each other and to mental health services. However, many people see themselves as friends, parents, sons or daughters, but not as 'carers': *'I didn't know I was a carer until I was told'* (carer, quoted in Repper et al., 2008, p. 426). While the notion of 'carer' may have been positive in highlighting the needs of those who find themselves in the position of providing care and support, it can also be unhelpful, as it suggests a polarised and non-reciprocal relationship between 'service user' and 'carer'. This oversimplification hides that fact that many people experiencing mental distress are themselves parents or provide care and support to others.

The term 'ally' may be more useful than 'carer' since, for people experiencing mental distress, the support that they need may often be as much emotional as it is practical – listening, spending time together and holding the hope that there will be light at the end of the tunnel. It is about being in a special relationship with the person, one that may comprise some very ordinary and everyday interactions, but may also involve, at times, an unusual degree of empathy, patience and commitment. Just 'being there' with someone who is mentally distressed can be very challenging but also very rewarding. It may require particular attention to communicating clearly and checking out, and involve encounters with strange (and sometimes frightening) perceptions and inner realities. Perhaps the hardest aspect is maintaining hope and connection while facing the (perhaps not just temporary) *'loss of the person you thought they were'* (carer, quoted in Repper et al., 2008, p. 425).

If friends and family members are going to be able to deal with such issues and feelings, they may, in turn, need to rely on wider networks of allies – and sharing responsibilities between a small team of allies is likely to provide a much more sustainable system of support that a reliance on just one person having to be there all the time for the person in distress (Copeland, 1997).

It is estimated that over 25% of people receiving treatment in acute inpatient settings, and nearly half of those using mental health services overall, are parents of dependent children (Bates and Coren, 2006). However, within routine approaches to psychiatric assessment, this crucial aspect of people's lives has often been ignored, so that people have not been supported in continuing in their parental roles (albeit accepting current limitations). Similarly, the needs of their children have often been overlooked in terms of:

- ensuring their care in their own right;
- maintaining quality contact with parents (visiting a parent on an adult psychiatric ward can be a terrifying experience, with no opportunity for dignified 'family time' together);
- explaining in an age-appropriate way what is going on; and
- looking at some of the specific issues that may have arisen if the child has taken on a 'young carer' role (Aldridge and Becker, 2003).

Family dynamics and relationship difficulties

Relationships, just like individuals, may become distressed, characterised by fracture, confusion, emotional distortion and irrationality, and can take on a self-destructive momentum of their own. This may apply both to individual relationships and also to relationship systems such as families.

In different ways, pioneers such as Bateson, Lidz and Laing sought to explain mental distress – and particularly psychosis – on the basis of dysfunctional family dynamics and communication patterns. However, some of this work was over-simplistic, implicitly constructing a parent (typically the mother) as 'schizophrenogenic' – as somehow having the power to induce 'schizophrenia' in their offspring. This is particularly unhelpful as it decontextualises the situation from any analysis of interactional patterns, and wider social pressures or constructions that may influence both family dynamics and the internal psychic dynamics of the person who may go on to experience psychosis.

This led to a very legitimate concern that such perspectives were leading to already overburdened families becoming caught up in a destructive discourse of blame, which tended only to make matters worse for all concerned. A consensus emerged which made this a 'no-go' area for research or exploration – and discourses that assumed biological causation became dominant. Within much of social psychiatry, it was seen as permissible to research how family dynamics and communication patterns could have a major impact on people's likelihood of relapse – once an initial 'biological' breakdown had occurred – but not to explore whether some of these selfsame dynamics might have contributed to a person's initial breakdown (Johnstone, 1999).

In revisiting the evidence that may link issues of family dynamics with the likelihood of breakdown and relapse, we must situate our discussion outside the parameters of the 'blame game'. Any search for blame can undermine both the clarity of our theoretical analysis, and our ability to engage therapeutically with all parts of a system which may need to recover if the person with mental distress is also to be enabled to recover. What may be much more helpful than the idea of blame is the Gestalt notion of 'response-ability' – recognising that we may (inadvertently) be contributing to difficulties, that we have choices in how we respond, and that we have the ability to act differently once we are clearer as to what is going on.

A range of research findings would suggest that, particularly for those who may already be more sensitive for genetic or other reasons, exposure to particular forms of relationship dynamics can contribute *both* to the likelihood of initial breakdown *and* subsequent relapse (Goldstein, 1985). In relation to childhood experience and its impact on mental health in adult life, a large-scale longitudinal study of adopted children in Finland has provided some of the most useful data (Tienari et al., 2004). Within this sample there were some children judged to be at high genetic risk (having first-degree relatives with a diagnosis of 'schizophrenia'). Overall, despite having to negotiate the attachment issues that go with separation from birth family and joining an adoptive family, those who moved into supportive adoptive family environments experienced an incidence of subsequent breakdown that was little different from that which would be expected in the general population – which suggests that positive family experiences can help to heal traumas and contribute to long-term resilience. However, nearly 5% of those brought up in a difficult family environment came to be diagnosed with 'schizophrenia' in adult life – and this proportion rose to 13% for those with genetic sensitivity.

The impact of mental distress on family and social relationships

Just as important as the processes whereby family dynamics may contribute to mental distress are the reciprocal processes whereby the mental distress of one individual may project outwards and impact on that person's relationships with those around. While they are going through the acute phase of a mental health crisis, a person may not be able to maintain their part in many social and family relationships. The familiar and taken-for-granted may suddenly become problematic for all concerned. Comfort and trust may suddenly be replaced by uncertainty and threat. Doubts and unresolved issues concerning a relationship may suddenly tumble out, but not in a way that may make them easy to resolve. Last-ditch defence mechanisms may result in conflicts and issues from the internal world becoming projected onto those around, so that a loved one may be transformed into an embodiment of evil or as a potentially murderous threat. This potential dislocation of relationships and identities should not be underestimated and can represent a trauma for all concerned – and family and other social systems may need time and support if they are to recover.

Where the distress is less acute, the impact upon relationships may be less dramatic, but can nevertheless be profound. Such changes, whether dramatic or more subtle, can be deeply challenging to many relationships. The mental distress of others can easily touch on one's own vulnerabilities and fears; it may be disruptive, not just in a practical sense, but in upsetting the terms of one's close relationships and impacting on one's own sense of self. These reactions may be located within and conditioned by wider social processes in which mental distress can be stigmatised and constructed as a threat (see Chapter 7), or where one may feel impelled to blame oneself or others for what has happened.

Sometimes the challenges posed by a person's mental distress to those close to them may be more than they are able to deal with: tension and conflict may escalate and relationships may break up and friends disappear. However, the contrary may also be true: some people may rise to the challenge, and may also find that they are moved by the experience in a very positive sense. They may discover new strengths and insights (both in relation to themselves and those that they care about), and relationships may become deeper, more honest and more accepting. Features which may enable relationships to endure and recover from mental distress include:

- a commitment to dialogue and co-operative activity, even when this is far from straightforward;
- unconditional acceptance;
- acknowledgement of pain and difficulty, *and* of positives and potentials;
- holding on, during bad times, to the expectation that there will be 'light at the end of the tunnel';
- an absence of patterns of blaming – either self or others;
- all parties having a number of potential sources of support so that no one is wholly dependent on another;
- external support and validation within wider social networks and professional systems.

While the person experiencing mental distress may be particularly vulnerable to tensions and discord within relationships, so may certain others, such as children. For example, if a parent is depressed, they may appear distant and unreachable as their emotional world shuts down – and hence may be temporarily unable to be there for their children. The research evidence suggests that parental mental health difficulties (including psychosis) do not necessarily have an adverse impact on children as long as they have good support from other relationships and they have the opportunity to talk about what is going on. However, if this is coupled with other factors, such as lack of social support, insensitive professional intervention or social stigmatisation, children may become troubled, anxious or guilty – and this may increase their chances of experiencing mental distress as adults (Evans and Fowler, 2008; Gopfort et al., 2004).

Social systems

Systems theory provides a framework for analysing the dynamics of the various family, social and work-based relationship groupings of which we are a part. Although much of early systems theory was located within a functionalist paradigm, more recent developments have taken it away from engineering-based metaphors of cybernetic regulation, so that it can connect better with ideas of identity and difference, social capital and, most importantly, power relations.

Systems may be defined as sets of interactive relationships which may vary in size, formality and permanence, that may be sensitive to external stresses and liable to develop internal conflicts and tensions (Polak, 1971). These distinct or overlapping systems set the terms of our main social relationships and the expectations around the roles we may play within them. Social systems are themselves located within wider social and cultural contexts which may be characterised by social divisions and inequalities, and these may be reproduced within the system in terms of power hierarchies or role expectations constructed around gender, age and other factors.

Within each system there are shared narratives which shape the system as a whole, giving it a collective identity in its dealings with the wider world, as well as constructing the various internal positions that system members may occupy. A group of work colleagues may be invited to see themselves as a 'team', or partners in a gay relationship may construct themselves as a 'married couple'. Such narratives may be contested, with alternative versions existing uneasily side by side. They may incorporate elements from wider social and cultural discourses, but may also contain idiosyncratic elements that resist dominant narratives. For example, a Black family may construct itself around mutually affirmative identities, providing a safe space away from dominant discourses of racial inferiorisation or abuse.

Central to the organisation of systems are the informal (and usually unstated) 'rules' which govern how system members function in relation to each other, and with the wider world beyond. They may be imposed or negotiated – or simply emerge through custom and practice – and may comprise:

- *Permitted and prescribed identities* – the various identities that system members may (have to) take on, both in relation to each other, and in relation to the outside world.
- *Norms/expectations* – how people believe they (and others) ought to act and present themselves.
- *Patterns of communication and interaction* – what can be expressed, how can it be expressed and by whom; how is closeness and distance regulated?
- *Boundary processes* – who is in and who is out, and how open is the system to interacting with the wider world?
- *The organisation of power and authority* – how are decisions made or contested; who has power over whom; in what ways are power relations limiting or productive?

These rules may be shaped by wider system narratives and also by prevailing discourses around age, gender, culture, and so on. They may also reflect internal interactions and adjustments within the system – which may, in turn, contribute to shaping and reshaping the wider system narratives.

Social systems, social support and social capital

Much of the time, system rules may work quite well for us, giving us taken-for-granted access to a certain level of support, resources and (perhaps) possibilities for emotional connection with other system members – all underpinned by some degree of shared understanding of our mutual obligations. As well as promoting possibilities for *co-operative* power, system rules may establish the basis whereby *protective* power may be deployed to safeguard those who may be vulnerable within the system. Membership of such systems may enable us to deal with the pressures or setbacks that might otherwise have an adverse impact on our mental health.

Family and other systems do not exist in isolation – to a greater or lesser degree they may be interconnected with other social systems (Germain & Glitterman, 1996). It is usually through our connections *within* systems that we can access *bonding* social capital, and it is often through the system's external connections that may that we can access *bridging* social capital. System narratives and rules can secure norms of trust, belonging and reciprocity which provide the discursive underpinnings for the successful operation of social capital (see Chapter 4). For many people, it can be family – extended as well as nuclear – that can be the primary route towards accessing social capital, whether it involves finding a reputable plumber, sorting out childcare, or arranging crisis support while someone is experiencing acute mental distress.

Issues and tensions within relationship systems

Membership of family and other social systems may not always be such a benign experience. As well as providing support, challenge and stimulation, they may also become locations of tension, conflict and, potentially, abuse and victimisation. This may result from the interaction of a range of factors, including the following.

Oppressive or collusive power relations

Families or other social systems may be subject to collective discrimination or 'othering' on the basis of their race, culture, inferior economic status or other identifying characteristic (such as having a family member with a disability). This can result in their being isolated from external sources of *co-operative* and *protective* power. In some instances, this external stress may also become internalised, with system members seeing each other negatively and taking their hurt and anger out on each other – and thereby losing out on possibilities for mutual support and *co-operative* power.

Alongside this, external social and cultural relations may establish a template, such as the normative form of the modern nuclear family, whereby internal family or group relations are to be constructed – although actual forms of organisation may also reflect internal issues and struggles. With these may come prevailing constructions of gender and age (and other aspects of identity) that may set the stage for internal hierarchies of power that may be *oppressive* or *protective*.

Victimisation and abuse may take place if certain individuals become isolated from external and internal relationships of *co-operative* power and where those in positions of relative *power over* fail to provide any viable organisation of *protective* power. Instead there may be an explicit or implicit arrangement of *collusive* power that ignores or even legitimates actions such as bullying or abuse, and serves to silence the voices of those who may become victimised. As we have seen, being subject to such *oppressive* actions on an ongoing basis can make us vulnerable to mental distress; so too can being situated as the powerless observer, unable to mobilise sufficient *protective* power to stop what is going on.

Unresolved conflicts and interpersonal defence mechanisms

In working with families of young adults with a diagnosis of 'schizophrenia', Theodore Lidz noted many instances of unresolved and ongoing discord (*'schism'*) – usually between the parents, but often with other family members being sucked in on each side. Alternatively, such issues might be covered over beneath an appearance of harmony – which could only be maintained by *'skewed'* family dynamics such as one parent effectively opting out and the other compensating by becoming over-involved, or where "one spouse passively acceded to the strange and even bizarre concepts of the more dominant spouse concerning ... how a family should live together (1975, p. 23). Set against such a relationship context, a person's unusual thoughts and utterances might make sense as responses to living with an underlying hostility that they are unable to control, and having to navigate between conflicting expectations and impossible demands.

Some patterns of unresolved tension, compensation or disengagement may be the legacy of trauma or abuse that can impact, not just upon one individual, but on their relationships with those around them. While sometimes, in the aftermath of such an event, informal system rules may change so that people may become closer and support each other, often people will not know how to cope with their own and each other's pain, and defence mechanisms such as denial or blaming may become embedded within system interactions. Sometimes, more powerful members of the system will project their unacceptable feelings on to less powerful members, perhaps pushing them into taking on the role of scapegoat. Alternatively, people may compensate by overprotecting the victim as a way of not having to face their own guilt or pain. Whatever may be the specific interpersonal defence mechanisms, the end result is likely to be a shift from a family or social group that was, by and large, functional to one which may be struggling badly and displaying multiple problems – and where one or more system members may come to experience mental health difficulties.

Expression of emotion

There is a substantial body of research within social psychiatry which looked at how exposure to particular patterns and emotional dynamics may influence the likelihood of relapse (Kuipers et al., 1992) and perhaps, by implication, initial breakdown. Rather unhelpfully, this type of interaction was labelled as high 'expressed emotion'. However, further research and refinement of the analysis showed that the clear and direct expression of emotions by others (including potentially challenging ones such as anger or sadness) has no adverse impact – as long as people clearly own their feelings, and articulate what their upset is about and to whom their feelings are directed.

Instead, it was found that what was most undermining to the mental health of those recovering from psychosis tended to be:

- *intrusiveness and over-involvement* – people fussing, worrying or taking over; not giving people the space to think and make decisions for themselves; or being emotionally dominating and demanding particular responses;
- *hostility* – including where this may be simmering or covert (perhaps better conceptualised as high *un*expressed emotion).

The over-involvement of other(s) and the intrusiveness of their interactions may make it hard for people to establish identities, boundaries and patterns of connection with others with which they are comfortable – which can be a particular issue for people who are having psychotic experiences. Such dynamics may be understand-able (if not entirely helpful) responses to the threats, uncertainties and sense of burden and duty which family and friends may associ-ate with caring for a person with mental distress – particularly if they themselves feel anxious or unsupported. However, such problematic relationship styles may also reflect patterns of interaction that may predate the onset of psychosis – and may reflect issues such as low self-esteem among those who find themselves in the position of carers (Kuipers et al., 2006). In such instances, it may be that family and friends may need as much support as the person with overt distress, if the whole system is to be enabled to recover and the underlying relationship issues are to be resolved.

Indirect or contradictory patterns of communication

Few families or social groups manage to communicate in ways that allow everyone to be heard and to have an equal voice, and for all communications to be clear and unambiguous. While many social systems nevertheless function reasonably well without such 'super communication', this may become an issue if they are also faced with particular challenges, stresses or internal tensions. If channels of communication are restricted or distorted, system members may find themselves unable to clarify or resolve issues, or negotiate between competing needs or demands – potentially becoming stuck in the sorts of patterns of discord or disengagement that were discussed above. Indirect or contradictory patterns of communication can become particularly problematic within a context of oppressive or collusive power relations, trapping those who are relatively powerless or vulnerable within impossible 'double binds' in which anything that they say or do turns out to be 'wrong' (Bateson et al., 1956).

Linking this to the 'expressed emotion' research, we may see how living within an atmosphere of hostility, particularly where negative feelings seem somewhat free-floating and are not owned, may also be potentially threatening to one's sanity: either one becomes super-capable at deciphering what may be going on, or one may start to get confused, perhaps assuming that somehow all these feelings may be directed towards oneself and that one is to blame for everything that is going wrong.

System instability and crisis

Where internal conflicts or external stresses cannot be resolved or managed satisfactorily, the system as a whole may become unstable and the existing system rules may become ineffective. Those in positions of relative power within the system may respond by rachet-ing up the existing control mechanisms, in a desperate attempt to maintain the status quo – with potentially adverse consequences both for the effective functioning of the system and for the mental health of particular individuals. Alternatively, there may come a point when existing system rules and control mechanisms cease to work and the system may enter a state of crisis and potential 'meltdown'.

The crisis may construct a particular system member as the 'problem' – typically someone who is particularly vulnerable and relatively powerless within the organisation of the system. They are likely to be identified as 'out of control' in some sense. However, from their point of view, they may have exhausted all 'sane' strate-gies for trying to resolve an increasingly unliveable situation – and their desperation may be directed outwards in forms of anti-social behaviour or inwards as mental distress.

When people come to experience mental distress, this may be both a form of protest against, and an attempt to cope within, a relationship system that is itself deeply problematic. As will be discussed in Chapter 9, it may be more productive to work to resolve the system issues that have led to the crisis, rather than seeking to treat a 'damaged' individual (Bridgett and Polak, 2003; Seikkula et al., 2003). Often, the person may find it relatively easy to resolve their distress once they are no longer trapped within a system of oppressive, collusive or conflictual relationships.

Summary of key points

- The concept of 'carer' is not necessarily helpful in mental health – the term 'ally' better describes the special personal relationship that people may need in order to recover.
- Membership of family and other social systems provides us with our main access to social support and social capital.
- Relationship difficulties can contribute to mental distress and vice versa – and both may stem from the impact of traumatic life events.
- Particular features of family and social systems that can contribute to mental distress include
  - oppressive or collusive power relations;
  - unresolved conflict and hostility – both overt and covert;
  - interpersonal defence mechanisms – such as denial and projection;
  - intrusiveness and over-involvement;
  - indirect or contradictory patterns of communication;
  - system instability and crisis.

Further reading

Gopfort, M., Webster, J., & Seeman, M. (eds) (2004). *Parental Psychiatric Disorder: Distressed Parents and Their Families.* Cambridge: Cambridge University Press.

Johnstone, L. (1999). Do families cause 'schizophrenia'? Revisiting a taboo subject. In C. Newnes, G. Holmes, & C. Dunn (eds), *This Is Madness.* Ross on Wye: PCCS Books.

Kuipers, L., Leff, J., & Lam, D. (1992). *Family Work for Schizophrenia.* London: Gaskell.

Repper, J., Grant, G., Nolan, M., & Enderby, P. (2008). Carers' experiences of mental health services and views about assessments. In T. Stickley & T. Basset (eds), *Learning About Mental Health Practice.* Chichester: Wiley.

7 | Social models of mental distress

As we saw in Chapter 2, the onset of mental distress marks a point on a continuum when particular experiences or patterns of response start to take over our overall functioning in a way that becomes problematic. It does not come as a 'bolt out of the blue' and, in this chapter, I will explore how various social factors may interact in the build-up towards an episode of mental distress – and how other factors, such as resilience and social capital, may protect us from going 'over the edge'. Such a model may be helpful in understanding what may underlie or trigger mental distress experiences and hence how best to target preventative and early intervention services (see Chapter 8).

There is much in common between the experience of people with mental distress and those who face other forms of disability. However, as a form of difference, mental distress can evoke particularly extreme forms of social reaction. Not only may people be patronised or excluded, but they may also be constituted as a threat to society, due to both an exaggerated (and misplaced) fear about their potential for violence, and an underlying concern around overt expressions of irrationality. Building upon theories of stigma and the social model of disability, I will develop a second model which looks at how mental distress may trigger a range of social consequences that can be as problematic as the distress experience itself.

Factors that increase the likelihood of mental distress

Personal vulnerability

In Chapter 5, we explored how we make adaptations in terms of our personality and our social functioning in response to particular life events and social circumstances. Where these enhance our personal efficacy and increase our capacity to resolve difficulties, they can lay the foundations for our ongoing resilience. However, our responses to (and internalisation of) oppressive or traumatic experiences may leave us vulnerable to the challenges posed by stresses and problems of living in later life.

Some adaptations, such as acquiring a negative sense of self or a suspicious orientation towards others, may impact upon our mental health by undermining our ability to deploy an active coping style and to sustain positive forms of social engagement. Other adaptations may take the form of defence mechanisms that 'click in' when we are faced with stress or difficulty and take us into a way of coping with (or shutting off from) the situation that is largely outside our conscious control. While such mechanisms may have made sense as survival strategies in early life, they may become problematic later on and contribute to our vulnerability.

Lifestyle issues

As we saw in Chapter 5, there can be mutually reinforcing connections between personality adaptations, coping strategies and the sort of lifestyle that we come to lead. Satisfying and stable lifestyles may contribute to our resilience and help us to stay linked in with wider networks of social capital and social support. Particularly problematic can be lifestyles that are chaotic, anti-social, self-destructive or overly stressful – and such lifestyles may have a very direct bearing on both the likelihood that we may encounter serious problems of living, and on our capability to deal with these.

It is often the interaction between a lifestyle issue and an adaptation that can tip someone over into an experience of mental distress – where either, on their own, would have been manageable. For example, a person may start to hear voices in response to a particular life event. Of itself, this may not be particularly problematic (as is the case for the majority of voice hearers – see Chapter 2). However, if the person also makes changes in their lifestyle, such as dropping out of social networks and avoiding close relationships, the two may become mutually reinforcing. Increased social isolation may create a gap which is filled by internal voices, and an increased intensity of voice-hearing experiences may make it harder to cope in social situations, leading to a greater recourse to social withdrawal. It is this interaction between the intra-psychic and the social which may start to define a pathway that may ultimately lead to mental distress or breakdown.

Issues and tensions within relationship systems

As we saw in Chapter 6, our location within family, work and other social relationships may provide us with much of our access to social support and social capital. However, our situation within particular relationships or relationship systems may also be potentially damaging to our mental health, particularly if we are relatively powerless within systems that are characterised by:

- oppression or unresolved conflicts;
- hostility or over-involvement;
- indirect or contradictory patterns of communication; or
- instability and crisis.

Being placed in such situations may undermine our sense of self, our efficacy, our confidence in forming attachments and our cognitive or emotional capabilities.

There can be patterns of reciprocal interaction in which our positioning within discordant or oppressive relationships may increase our personal vulnerability, and the personality adaptations that we make may increase our chances of finding ourselves within such relationship situations.

Stress

In our daily lives, we may be subject to a range of stress factors. These are circumstances which tend to push us off balance and challenge our existing range of coping strategies and social supports – resulting in a (temporary) state of unease. There are no absolutes as to what may constitute a stress – what we may find stressful can depend on our particular adaptations, lifestyles and social situations.

Some current stresses may be similar to the social factors that may have contributed to personal vulnerability – such as loss or abuse. Where a current stress mirrors past experience, it may have a particularly devastating impact as it may feed into an existing area of vulnerability – it may become the 'straw that breaks the camel's back'. Stresses may also arise out of conflicting pressures and expectations, such as the demands of work and family, or growing up within the parallel cultures of being Asian and British.

Both over- and under-stimulation can be problematic: social isolation and unemployment can be stressful, as can feeling overburdened with work or other responsibilities. Thresholds of over- and under-stimulation can vary considerably between people and, for some, there may be quite a fine line between the two. This would seem to be a particularly important issue for people who are vulnerable to psychosis, where managing levels of stimulation in order to maintain the right balance can be key to maintaining wellbeing.

Stress can arise in relation to life transitions that involve renegotiating identities and establishing new networks of social and family support. Research has shown that it is not always transitions that may be perceived negatively which are stressful: new beginnings as well as endings may be hard to navigate (Dohrenwend et al., 1978). Examples of transitions that may be stressful include:

- leaving home;
- separation and divorce;
- partnership and marriage;
- moving house;
- changing job;
- redundancy;
- having a baby;
- children growing up;
- retirement.

Many people are able to connect the onset of their mental distress with one or more of such stress factors. It is no coincidence that first breakdowns are most common at particular points in the life cycle when major adjustments may have to be made – such as late adolescence, early parenthood or middle age.

Oppression, humiliation and shame

Issues of power and control can have a major impact on what may be experienced as stressful. People may cope and even thrive on lifestyles that involve very demanding work or caring responsibilities, as long as they feel in charge of what they take on and valued for what they do. Where this can become problematic is when people are subject to oppressive power relations that give them no choice as to what they have to do, or force them to take on roles that are demeaning or exploitative.

Just as vulnerability may result from internalising past experiences of oppression, so current experiences of disadvantage, discrimination or injustice may contribute very directly to our unease if we do not have strategies for challenging or resisting them. Certain types of experience would seem to be particularly toxic – such as where one is put down or excluded, and one's attempts to stand up for oneself (or others) result in 'failed struggle' and humiliation (Gilbert and Allen, 1998; Selten and Cantor-Graae, 2007). This humiliation may relate to specific (and sometimes very public) experiences of defeat or shame – such as rape or racist abuse. More insidiously, people may take on a sense of humiliation if they fail to live up to particular family or cultural expectations, or if their identity comes to be seen as 'spoiled' (Goffman, 1963). Whatever the circumstances, experiences of humiliation and shame can be an important trigger for mental health difficulties.

Process models: how factors interact

The Stress–Vulnerability Model (Zubin and Spring, 1977) provides a useful starting point for conceptualising how past and present factors may come together to contribute to mental breakdown or subsequent relapse (see Figure 7.1). The greater the underlying vulnerability, the smaller the current stress may need to be before it triggers an experience of mental distress, and vice versa. Although sometimes used rather simplistically to suggest how underlying biological vulnerabilities could be triggered into full-blown 'illnesses' by psychosocial stresses, this model potentially allows for vulnerabilities to be of social as well as biological origin.

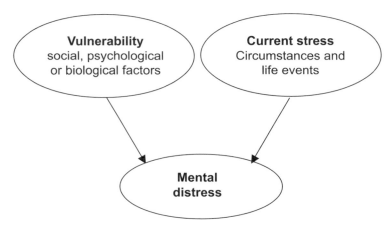

Figure 7.1 The Stress–Vulnerability model

Along somewhat similar lines, Kinderman (2005) suggests a 'Mediating Psychological Processes' Model. In this, social circumstances (such as poverty or social deprivation), life events (such as abuse or victimisation) and any biological predispositions are seen as interacting in ways that induce disturbed psychological processes – which then constitute 'a final common pathway' in the development of mental distress (see Figure 7.2).

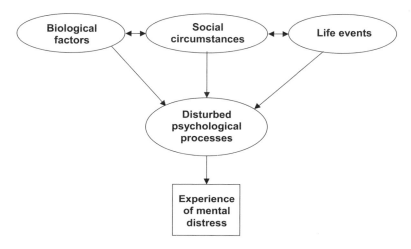

Figure 7.2 Mediating Psychological Processes Model

Source: Adapted from Kinderman et al., 2008, pp. 93–103.

Both models provide useful frameworks whereby to see how different factors may come together to trigger an experience of mental distress. However, they do not cover all the aspects that may be important within a more comprehensive social model, such as:

- the potential role of positive factors, such as resilience, social capital and social support, in averting the possibility of mental distress;
- lifestyle and relationship issues that may be just as important a part of a 'final common pathway' as 'disturbed psychological processes';
- the specific impact of power relations in constructing situations of oppression, humiliation and entrapment.

Unease

In our conceptualisation of the processes that may lead on to mental distress, it is important to identify intermediate stages – 'decision points' at which a weighing up of the different factors affecting a person's situation may help us to understand why they may or may not become impelled towards mental distress. A crucial stage is that of *unease*: how a person may be experiencing a situation that has become a serious problem of living. Their ability to respond may be influenced both by their particular areas of vulnerability and resilience, and by their social situation, including their access to social capital and potentially supportive personal relationships.

Unlike the idea of 'disturbed psychological processes', the concept of unease gives the person ownership of their experience: it is *their* unease in relation to *their* situation that needs to be understood, not any imposed diagnosis of pathology. It also signals the possibility of resolution rather than the inevitability of decline into mental distress – and suggests a point at which supportive interventions might be helpful in averting a full-blown mental health crisis, through addressing causes of stress and oppression, and mobilising people's access to social support systems and resources.

Typically, our unease may relate to our current social experience – stresses, relationship tensions, humiliation, and so on – and also to the re-emergence of unresolved issues from the past. While our defence mechanisms may have (just about) contained feelings of rage or hurt that could not have been expressed at the time, these feelings tend not to go away completely. Instead, they may turn into an emotional 'hot potato' that becomes harder and harder to hold inside and which has the potential to erupt into the here-and-now with uncontrolled force (the 'return of the repressed'). Often, the timing of this re-emergence is not coincidental but connects with aspects of current experience.

Resilience, social support and social capital

Faced with unease and more challenging problems of living, people may be able to resolve this by drawing upon both their internalised resilience and active coping styles (see Chapter 5), and whatever external supports and opportunities may be available to them (their social capital). The latter may be particularly important in dealing with the sense of social failure that may result from experiences of humiliation and shame.

As we shall see in Chapter 9, social relationships are central to people's recovery; they are also equally important in enabling people to resolve their unease and deal with their problems of living. If social support is to be mobilised, this can depend on both the person, in terms of their attachment style and cognitive social capital, and on their social environment: their current positioning within confiding and supportive personal relationships, and their wider access to bonding and bridging forms of social capital (see Chapter 4). Where both are in evidence, prospects may look good. However, social isolation, or a lack of confidence in engaging with others, may result in people being catapulted into a (perhaps familiar) status of victimhood or disengagement that may then lead on to experiences of mental distress.

The build-up to mental distress: entrapment, isolation and escalation of defence mechanisms

A concept that may better capture the dynamics of the 'final common pathway' is that of entrapment (Gilbert and Allen, 1998): finding ourselves caught in a situation where options and opportunities are closed off and we are unable to resolve or deal with our unease. We may face increasing powerlessness due to external factors such as oppressive relationships and expectations, social isolation or the disintegration of personal relationships, and the continuing impact of particular stresses. Some of this process of entrapment may also be internal: escalations of defence mechanisms may start to close in and reduce our capacity for active coping and engagement, often by distorting our contact with, and appraisal of, external realities. Specific complaints, such as hearing voices, may be seen as representing 'a socio-emotional conflict' that has become 'internalised ... without an available solution in the daily life situation' (Pennings and Romme, 2000, p. 42).

The concept of entrapment highlights the pivotal role played by power relations – both external and internalised – in creating the conditions which lead to breakdown. In turn, this suggests that interventions and supports that address oppression and disempowerment are likely to be crucial in working to avert or resolve mental health crises – and that forms of treatment or care that (however inadvertently) feed into an exacerbation of powerlessness are likely to make an already desperate situation worse.

Building on the process models discussed above, Figure 7.3 offers a more comprehensive model of the factors that may contribute to, or guard against, the onset of mental distress. Although biological factors may have influenced people's sensitivity to particular stresses and adverse social experiences, there is little evidence that they directly trigger someone's breakdown – hence this model is primarily social in its conception.

From this model, we may see how experiences of distress may have quite a complex history. In most instances, no single 'cause' can be identified. Instead, we have a number of social and personal factors interacting over time which may, or may not, lead to a point of breakdown. Such a process of cumulative interactions can be seen in M.L.'s account of her experience (Box 7.1). Using a social model to explore such journeys can make it much easier to identify points where some additional support or intervention might make a crucial difference in the path that is followed.

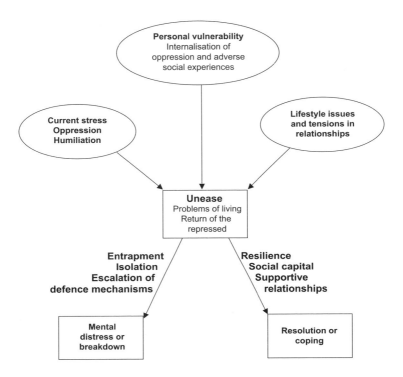

Figure 7.3 Social model (1): the build-up to mental distress

While medication may have some (temporary) value in buffering people from current stress, it is predominantly social issues that may need to be addressed if the painful journey from unease to break-down is to be avoided.

Box 7.1   M.L.'s story

'I have been sexually abused. I think when I was three years old, by a much older cousin … To me he seemed very big … We moved to England when I was seven years old … In the streets, old people … said to me 'Dirty nigger' or 'Go home monkey'. I was shocked. My parents did not allow me to play outside. As they gained confidence, they allowed me to go outside. But by then I did not have anyone to play with. That was terrible as well.

I was sexually abused again when I was nine. We lived in a shared house. The man upstairs lived with his family … He gave me the warning 'Don't tell your parents' and I did not …

When I was 12 ... I heard a terrible laugh coming from the garden. It sounded like witches laughing ... I prayed to God ... to make him stop that noise. My first experience of hearing voices in my head was God answering back to let me know that it was my fear, and that I had to stop being afraid in the dark ...

At the age of 12 I met my ex-husband. He was my first real boyfriend. When I was 16 I got pregnant twice, and both times I lost the baby. My mother decided that I was not going to have babies. She told me to use the douche and I obeyed ...

The twins were born when I was 18. When I got pregnant, I was still not married. But this time I wanted the babies, and did not listen to my mother. I married when I was 20, and I wanted another baby. We then quarrelled quite a bit, but I still wanted another baby ...

When Sam was three years old, I got into trouble at my work. I am a childcare worker. One of the nurses tried to prove that I was aggressive, and the rest of the staff backed her up ... When I talked, they thought I was too emotional ...

I needed to get away from my husband. Not that he was horrible, but I was in too much pain. The reason that I went away in the first place was that I had too much anger in me. It was a question of either letting it out and taking the consequences, or fighting to keep it in. And I chose to fight to keep it in, in the right and proper way ...

I started to work again, but after a year I had the same kind of trouble. Racial problems ... I had to stop working because at my work they wanted me to reply to a letter of grievance (this caused the first breakdown) ...

I knew I had to get better because of the letter of grievance that I had to respond to so I could start working again. My wise cousin helped me with it ... At my work, the letter was accepted and understood. They decided to organise a racial awareness course ... After the racial awareness course I went to work again. Things changed and I felt more accepted by colleagues ...

The second period of illness was longer than the first one ... I smashed windows and was sectioned for 28 days. I was hearing voices all over the place ...

My problem was that I could not be myself living in a country that does not accept black people. But through the voices I found myself – my identity, which was everything to do with my racial history and my own past. The memory of my abuse stayed ...'

Source: (M.L., in Romme and Escher, 1993, pp. 122–4). Reproduced with permission.

In her narrative, M.L. is able to pick out connections between her distress experiences and both adverse social circumstances and particular abusive and humiliating life events – both in the past (contributing to her vulnerability) and in the present. Against a background in which there is little evidence of supportive personal relationships, the positive impact of her cousin helping her in her response to the grievance stands out. This enabled her to be heard in relation to her experience of racism at work – which, in turn, brought about a resolution of her immediate problem of living. However, other issues remained to fuel her unease (including memories of her abuse) – and this intervention did not, on its own, prove sufficient to avert her increasing social isolation and emerging mental distress.

The trauma of mental breakdown

A recurrent theme from recovery narratives is that people may need to recover, not just from any traumatic issues that may have contributed to their mental distress, but also from the trauma arising from breakdown itself (Deegan, 1988, 1989). As we saw in Chapter 3, trauma involves the dislocation of our attachments, identities and sense of self as a result of experiences that are frightening and beyond our control. In this sense, an episode of mental distress can be similarly jarring – both for the person and for those around them. However, while distress experiences may be potentially dislocating in their own right, it is often the social responses to mental breakdown that can be most traumatising.

What may make a difference, as with other forms of trauma, is the quality of supportive relationships that a person may have at the time that they experience a breakdown. If others are able to accept and be with the person while they are distressed, the level of rupture and trauma may be minimised. However, within a wider environment that may be dominated by discourses of fear and stigmatisation, such relationships may prove hard to sustain – and the person may find that they become distanced from those to whom they were close by barriers of guilt, fear or blame. Such consequences can only serve to escalate the impact of the trauma and make it much harder for it to be resolved.

Unfortunately, many conventional service responses, including hospitalisation and the use of compulsion, may serve to exacerbate what is already a very difficult situation. Family and friends are often marginalized from processes of treatment and care, thereby magnifying the potential for rupture of key attachments, and taking away potential supports for identities that may already be feeling uncertain and fragile.

People from black and minority ethnic communities may find hospitalisation a particularly alienating or traumatising experience – being removed from cultural familiarities and potentially also being exposed to racism or abuse from other patients or staff. Research has consistently shown how African and African Caribbean people may be subject to far higher levels of compulsory treatment, overmedication and coercive procedures such as seclusion and restraint (Browne, 2009; Keating, 2002) – all of which may add to their experience of traumatisation.

Labelling and stigma

Within particular cultural and historical settings, there can be demarcations between who is to be considered 'normal' or 'deviant'. Those who intentionally or unintentionally violate social codes may be subject to some form of social sanction. However, it is the ways in which ideas of difference are constructed within the social mainstream, rather than anything inherently 'wrong' about those who may be excluded, which can determine who becomes labelled as deviant (Becker, 1963). Once given this label, subsequent social interactions may tend to reinforce this – and people may easily come to internalise it as part of their sense of self.

Goffman's concept of stigmatisation has found particular resonance with the experience of people with mental distress who have found their social identities 'discredited' by social attitudes that reduce their status 'from a whole and usual person to a tainted, discounted one' (1963, p. 3). Actions or presentations, such as talking back to one's voices, walking with an unusual gait, losing attention easily, or appearing excitable or depressed, are not in themselves harmful or anti-social; it is only through processes originating within the social mainstream that these become constructed as deviant or 'discreditable'.

Underpinning stigmatisation are relations of unequal power (Link and Phelan, 2001) – with the social mainstream acting *collusively* to construct people with mental distress within a category of 'otherness' that renders them shameful and legitimates discrimination against them. Within popular discourse, many labels attached to people with mental distress can be straightforwardly abusive (such as 'nutter' or 'loony'). Alongside this, people may be subjected to a repertoire of demeaning or marginalizing responses, not just from the wider community but also from colleagues, friends and family members, such as urging the person to 'snap out of it' or withdrawing from them if their behaviour seems impossible to understand (Thornicroft, 2006).

Proponents of medical approaches have argued that it helps to 'normalise' mental distress if we see it as 'an illness like any other physical illness'. However, such a strategy has not successfully challenged wider social, media and political discourses. Instead, the more mental distress is understood biologically, the more people tend to be seen as fundamentally 'different' and the more the public seeks to become socially distanced from them (Read et al., 2006). Furthermore, medical diagnosis has provided a ready vocabulary by which to 'other' people with mental health difficulties, and labels such 'schizophrenic' or 'psychopath' simply re-emerge within popular discourse or media headlines as dehumanised identities such as 'schizo' or 'psycho'.

It can be easy for people to acquiesce to the labels that they are given, accepting the inferiorisation and social exclusion that goes with them – either as if this is inevitable, or, more perniciously, as if it is all their fault:

> *It's not until you have experienced stigma that you realise how important and how discriminated against and how bad and how guilty you can feel about having a mental health problem. Being seen as different is not good for you.* (service user, quoted in Alexander, 2008)

Particularly due to their state of powerlessness and the loss of more positive social identities, they may find that their (already fragile) self-concept becomes conflated with a medical diagnosis: they may lose their personhood and take on an identity such as 'schizophrenic'. In turn, they may internalise a deep personal sense of shame, perhaps accompanied by guilt or fears about their supposed dangerousness.

This may be seen as a form of internalised oppression that mirrors other ways in which oppression may have been internalised, potentially exacerbating their mental distress. The internalisation and enactment of a stigmatised identity can result in:

- alienation from self and others;
- endorsing or 'buying in' to mental illness stereotypes; and
- social withdrawal (Sibitz et al., 2009).

There can be particular issues around stigma in minority communities: people can face the 'double jeopardy' of discrimination within the social mainstream on the basis of, say, their ethnicity, but also find that they are shunned or seen as shameful within their own communities on account of their mental distress – and there may be particular pressure to hide signs of distress for fear of bringing shame or discredit on family or community.

It is important to recognise that processes of stigmatisation do not just affect the person with mental distress: family and friends can get caught up in what Goffman termed 'stigma by association'. They are seen as infected by the shame of mental health difficulties and are also to be shunned or looked down upon. They may feel blamed (explicitly or implicitly) for having caused what has happened, or for failing to keep the community 'safe' from mental distress – and this sense of blame may come not just from the wider community, but also from interactions with professionals. Ultimately, this can lead to whole families being targeted with verbal abuse, harassment or even physical violence:

> *I had dog mess pushed through my letterbox, closely followed by paint stripper thrown over my door causing a lot of damage that took weeks to sort out.* (carer, quoted in Thornicroft, 2006, p. 12)

What is so special about mental distress? The disorderly subject and modern societies

A distinguishing feature of modern societies and their social and economic regulation is their foundation upon principles of rationalism (contrasting with more traditional societies where expressions of intuition or spiritual inspiration could be highly valued). As we saw in Chapter 4, in order to be recognised and participate as a citizen, one has to appear a coherent, consistent and, above all, rational subject.

It is in this context that mental distress may be seen to have posed particular problems for modernity – appearing more challenging to the social order than other more 'rational' acts of deviance such as criminality. Conducting oneself on the basis of apparently irrational insights, or overwhelming or volatile emotions, could be 'deemed inimical to society or the state – indeed could be regarded as a menace to the proper workings of an orderly, efficient, progressive, rational society' (Porter, 1987, p. 15). As Ernest Becker points out, at an even more basic level, what can appear most problematic, in terms of engaging with the discourses of modern living, 'is the person who renounces all zest for life in the game we are so dedicatedly playing; it unnerves us that someone can be so indifferent to everything we cherish' (1972, p. 140).

Thus mental distress may be seen as subversive – potentially undermining the appearance of rationality, and the ideology of individual achievement, that underpin the organisation of modern societies. In order to protect against this threat, there has been substantial investment in the 'helping' professions whose job it is to neutralise or correct any emergence of irrationality (Foucault, 1967) – either by banishing the mentally distressed to asylums or, more recently, by defining their distress as an 'illness' and using medication or other strategies to contain it within the community.

Paradoxically, it may not be the difference between 'mad' and 'normal' that is most problematic: it may actually be the potential for commonality of experience. We may fear that contact with others' mental distress may make us rather too aware of the fragility of our own 'sanity' through finding 'some of that distress in ourselves'; indeed, for many of us, 'those echoes … can still be too much to bear, prompting us to turn away' (Barker et al., 1999, p. 9).

The psychoanalytic concept of projection may be helpful here in showing how we may avoid the unacceptable in ourselves by identifying it in others – and the vehemence of our hostility towards them may be an indicator of our fear that we may actually be like them. This can start to explain what may be driving the apparently excessive and demonising responses that people with mental distress may receive from family, friends or the wider community.

In recent years, coinciding with the switch to policies of care in the community, a new mechanism for maintaining a separation between 'us' and 'them' has emerged in the form of a discourse around risk and dangerousness that has been fanned by media and government alike (Walsh, 2009) – although, as we shall see in Chapter 10, this has no basis in reality, as the proportion of homicides committed by people with mental distress has actually fallen. People with mental distress have become constructed as an 'alien menace' that is 'lurking in the shadows' (Laurance, 2003). In this way, deeper anxieties about our own irrationality and distress may be transmuted into an exaggerated fear of a dangerous 'other': the woman on the bus who talks to her voices is not to be shunned for the subversiveness of her irrationality but because this somehow means that she is a 'danger' to ordinary people.

Service responses, stigma and discrimination

Mental health services may inadvertently serve to increase people's experience of stigma and discrimination. People may find it harder to resist being engulfed by the label of 'mental illness' if they are admitted to hospital, with all its associated routines of medicalisation (Sibitz et al., 2009). Internalisation of negative identities may result from being implicitly labelled as dangerous through practices of risk assessment and risk management.

Alongside this, 'high-profile' forms of intervention, such as the involvement of the police in compulsory admissions, may also identify people in negative ways within their immediate neighbourhood or community.

Particular issues arise for members of Black and minority ethnic communities who may be subject to institutional discrimination within mental health services (Keating, 2002). Attitudes towards African and African Caribbean people that originated in slavery can still permeate modern psychiatric practice (Ferns, 2005); they may face assumptions that that they are impulsive, dangerous and incapable of managing their own mental functioning – thereby justifying excessive use of detention, force and overmedication (Browne, 2009), and a correspondingly limited access to 'talking therapies'. People from Asian communities may experience more subtle forms of discrimination resulting from a legacy of colonialism – perhaps with more spiritual worldviews and belief systems being seen as inferior to the 'scientific' basis of Westernised mental health services. The impact of such oppressive treatment within mental health services may be coupled with stigma within their own communities – and sometimes a sense that they have brought public shame upon family or community groupings that were already struggling to attain 'respectability' within a mainstream society that saw them as inferior.

The Social Model of Disability

In common with other disabled groups, people with mental distress face discrimination in areas such as employment and housing (Sayce, 2000) and find themselves excluded from a whole variety of valued social roles within family and community. However, the nature and extent of this can be particularly extreme when people's difficulties relate to mental health.

One framework for understanding how stigmatisation may impact upon people – and how this may be contested politically – has been the Social Model of Disability (Oliver, 1996). It introduced a conceptual separation between a person's physiological *impairment* and how they may be *disabled* in terms of their social and economic participation. It challenged the dominant discourse in which a person's social and physical environment had been taken as given, and the person, and their failure to be 'normal', was constructed as the problem, thereby inviting responses of self-blame, and feeding into the idea that impairment should be viewed as a 'tragedy'.

The Social Model of Disability suggests that what can be disabling is not so much the impairment itself, but the social (and physical) barriers that may be placed in the way of people's participation. 'Able' people's responses may be framed by a construction of 'normality' (and a representation of impairment) that can put down, patronise or exclude those who fall outside its definition. This perspective shifts the focus of intervention from the *person* to their *social situation* and, in particular, to processes of 'othering' and discrimination. It foregrounds issues of social identities: how may people claim positive identities that value their difference and allow them to adopt a personhood that that is no longer conflated with their impairment?

In many ways, the Social Model of Disability is relevant to people with mental distress, who may often find that societal and professional responses to their distress can be at least as problematic as the distress itself. However, its application is not entirely straightforward. One issue for people with mental distress is the implication of constructing their distress as an 'impairment' – a perspective which may implicitly reinforce the idea of it being a 'chronic illness' rather than a response to adverse social experiences from which recovery may be possible. So, although the model provides a welcome focus on changing the mainstream so that it is more accessible and accepting, this needs to be balanced with an emphasis on enabling people's journeys of personal change and recovery (see Chapter 9).

There may be strong parallels between the sorts of social experiences that may have originally contributed to someone's mental distress, and the oppressive and exclusionary social responses that they may now be suffering as a result of it. Stigmatisation may further damage their social identities, ways of relating, sense of self and emotionality, and hence trigger ever more extreme defence mechanisms and exacerbate the severity of their mental distress. We may therefore need to reformulate the Social Model of Disability in relation to mental health. Instead of facing just the 'double whammy' of impairment and socially imposed disability, people with mental health difficulties tend to face a 'triple whammy' in which they have to contend with not just their original distress experiences, but also potentially extreme responses of stigmatisation that may then, in turn, exacerbate their level of mental distress.

Adverse social consequences: social exclusion and dislocation of family and personal relationships

Figure 7.4 starts to map out how social responses of stigma and discrimination may result in social exclusion and dislocation of family and personal relationships – a potentially sudden loss of access to social capital. In turn, this may exacerbate the traumatic impact of the experience of mental distress on someone's already fragile sense of self-identity, perhaps leading them to internalise a sense that they are 'shameful'. These various social consequences may be seen to constitute an additional layer of trauma, stress and humiliation that is likely to create further unease and problems of living. In this way, we have a vicious circle which the social consequences of mental distress may be disabling, and this may both exacerbate people's mental distress and make it much harder for them to recover.

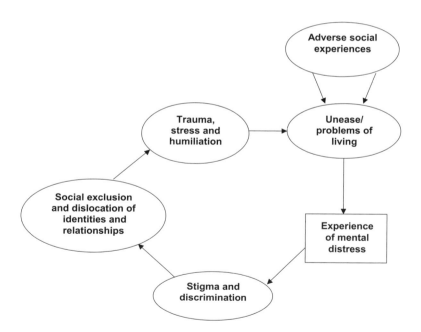

Figure 7.4 Social model (2): adverse social consequences of mental distress

The UK government report on social exclusion (Social Exclusion Unit, 2004) assembles a wide array of evidence as to the areas of people's lives in which they are likely to face exclusion or discrimination resulting from an experience of mental distress. What can be surprising is both the speed at which these losses can come about and the extent to which all areas of people's lives can be affected.

A person may find that they are suddenly stripped of particular roles within family or other settings, and they may find themselves excluded from important conversations and decision-making processes. They may no longer be seen as a responsible parent or treated as a spouse – and, while some changes to roles and expectations may be necessary for the good of all parties, they may find that others have acted unilaterally. For example, caring responsibilities may be removed without consultation or negotiation.

Out of all disabled groups, people with mental distress are least likely to be able to find employment (*ibid.*), and there is widespread evidence of discriminatory attitudes among employers (Read and Baker, 1996). Recent evidence from Britain suggests that, once people with an episode of mental distress have been out of work for over six months, over 50% will never find paid employment again (Office of National Statistics, 2003). For some people, specific stresses associated with their work environment may have contributed to their emerging distress – and therefore returning to work in the same environment may be problematic (although requesting reasonable adjustments under disability rights legislation may provide a useful basis for renegotiating this). For others, their workplace may provide supports and statuses that are very important for their wellbeing – and losing this may simply add to their overall experience of loss and dislocation.

As was discussed in Chapter 4, accessing informal social supports and resources through networks of social capital can be an important component that underpins wellbeing and resilience. However, during periods of mental distress, when one may have greatest need to call upon these, one may find that these networks are no longer available. Perhaps particularly where bonds and bridges may be relatively superficial, the stigma associated with mental distress may simply result in doors being closed. Alongside this, the distress experience itself may undermine people's confidence in mobilising their cognitive social capital. They may see themselves as useless, bad or undeserving of others' support – or have simply lost the drive and confidence to pick up the telephone. However, as network links are broken or fade away, it becomes much harder for social capital to be remobilised and people may become unhelpfully dependent on mental health services as a substitute for this.

Acceptance and recognition

People do not always experience discriminatory or disabling responses from everyone that they encounter. Many recovery narratives give a prominent place to a special someone – friend, family member or member of staff (often junior and untrained) – who stood by them through the darkest moments of their journey and continued to treat them with respect and understanding. At a more general level, public attitudes are always changing – although not always in very consistent directions. One survey found that, of those who were in work and were 'out' about their mental health difficulties, two-thirds described colleagues as always or very often accepting (Mental Health Foundation, 2002) – suggesting that positive experiences of contact and connection can be the best antidote to stigma.

Acceptance and recognition start with the positive acknowledgement of difference (Trivedi, 2008) and a valuing of the person and the experiential journey along which they are going, however strange some of this may seem. Crucially, it involves moving out of the *collusive* power relations of stigmatisation that can be so pervasive, and opening up opportunities for *co-operative* power, shared struggle and dialogue between those who are experiencing mental distress and those around them, including the practitioners who are involved in their support. As will be discussed in Chapter 9, it is often these experiences of acceptance and connection that link to positive turning points in people's recovery journeys.

Summary of key points

- The build-up to mental distress generally involves the interaction of
  - personal vulnerability;
  - lifestyle issues and tensions in relationship systems;
  - current stress, oppression and humiliation.
- Our unease may relate both to current problems of living and the re-emergence of unresolved past issues.
- Resilience and access to social support and social capital can help us to resolve our unease so that it does not turn into mental distress.

- The 'final common pathway' into mental distress generally involves experiences of entrapment and an escalation of defence mechanisms.
- The experience of mental breakdown can be traumatic – but the degree of trauma depends on the dislocation of social supports and interpersonal relationships.
- Stigma can play a major part in exacerbating both people's social exclusion and their mental health difficulties.
- Alienating and discriminatory service responses can add to the experience of trauma and impact of stigma – particularly for members of Black and ethnic minority communities.

further reading

Sayce, L. (2000). From psychiatric patient to citizen. *Overcoming Discrimination and Social Exclusion.* Basingstoke: Palgrave Macmillan.

Tew, J. (ed.) (2005). *Social Perspectives in Mental Health.* London: Jessica Kingsley.

Thornicroft, G. (2006). *Shunned: Discrimination Against People With Mental Illness.* Oxford: Oxford University Press.

8 | Early intervention and crisis resolution

Some particularly promising areas of service development in recent years have been in relation to early intervention and crisis resolution. There is an increasing body of evidence that 'getting in early' can pay dividends in minimising the social losses that may attach to mental distress, thereby making it easier for people to recover.

Holistic models of early intervention and crisis resolution give considerable weight to the social aspects of people's situations – understanding difficulties within the context of family and other key social systems, such as education, employment and social networks. In this chapter, I will look in more detail at how social support and interventions can contribute to effective practice – both in engaging proactively to minimise the potentially disabling impact of an emerging mental health crisis, and in resolving the personal and contextual issues that may be contributing to it.

Some more innovative services have been developed by, or in collaboration with, people with direct experience of mental distress (Stastny and Lehmann, 2007). Based on principles of peer support (and challenge), they aim to provide an ethos of collaborative engagement that is very different from the paternalism or coercive authority that is inherent within many conventional psychiatric services.

Early intervention

As we have seen, most experiences of mental distress are preceded by a period of build-up of increasing unease, and the onset of mental distress is not some sudden and immediately recognisable event, but a gradual exacerbation of certain problematic patterns of feeling, thinking or behaviour to the point at which a person's sense of personal agency and their ability to function within their social context become compromised. While this is going on, the person concerned (and those around them) may have limited awareness of what is happening – particularly if this is their first experience of mental distress. They may therefore tend to struggle on as best they can, using whatever coping strategies are available to them, until they reach a point of crisis.

Unfortunately, this period of 'struggling on' may be at some considerable cost in terms of increasingly strained relationships or loss of social roles – perhaps dropping out of employment or education. In turn, all of this may serve further to undermine their mental health. Quite often, a deterioration in people's social functioning may precede any more overt presentation of mental distress. It is suggested that the longer that incipient mental distress goes unrecognised, the greater the adverse social, psychological and physiological impact can be, making recovery potentially much longer and harder (Birchwood et al., 1998). Studies have shown that catching this as early as possible, through more effective screening and early intervention services, can result in reduced hospitalisation and better outcomes (Fowler et al., 2009; Power et al., 2007).

Recent data from one service suggests not just a dramatic fall in admissions and an equally dramatic fall in the use of compulsion, but also that people retain more hopefulness and greater levels of social participation – evidenced by a much lower incidence of attempted suicide and a substantial increase in family involvement and participation in employment or education and training (see Table 8.1).

Table 8.1 Outcomes – Worcestershire Early Intervention Service

	National audit data	Worcestershire Early Intervention Service 2008 (n = 106)
Admitted to hospital with first episode psychosis (%)	80	17.5
Admitted using Mental Health Act (%)	50	10
Family involved (%)	49	84
In employment/education/ training (%)	8–18	56
Suicide attempted (%)	48	7

Source: selected outcome data from Smith and Shiers, 2010, p. 33. Reproduced with permission.

Primarily because of reduced bed usage and earlier return to gainful employment, economic evaluations of early intervention services have shown that providing a comprehensive range of services to help people to deal with their personal and social issues is better value than a conventional service that is primarily based on medication and hospital admissions (McCrone et al., 2006).

Developing awareness of mental health issues

The greatest barrier to averting mental distress – or minimising its severity – is the stigma and misinformation which can surround mental health issues and people's lack of confidence in being able to respond to such issues in supportive ways.

School-based initiatives to promote wellbeing aim to equip children better in terms of fostering their capabilities in talking about emotional issues and in sharing and solving problems. However, there is still a long way to go in public education in terms of how to support someone if they start to show signs that they are not coping, including how to access professional help if this may be necessary. There may be value in more generalised activities that promote mental health awareness among communities – including minority communities – and also more targeted initiatives among those who may be more at risk of developing mental distress, such as young people leaving the care system or victims of sexual abuse.

Detection and screening

A key component to early intervention is early detection of mental distress, picking up when someone has started to move on from a situation of everyday unease (which they may potentially be able to resolve) to one where they are starting to show signs of mental distress. Typically, they may not be in contact with any specialist mental health service – perhaps because they may not identify their experience as a mental health issue or because of the fear and stigma attached to any mental health label. It is more likely that their deteriorating mental or emotional state might be noticed by family or friends – or by other professionals such as teachers, general practitioners or childcare social workers.

The ability to offer an early response can be undermined where mental health services are hard to access or appear unwelcoming. There can be particular issues for people from Black and minority ethnic communities: many people report that their concerns are not taken seriously until situations have deteriorated – and then 'no response' may quickly switch to 'over-response', often accompanied by excessive force and coercion.

It is in order to address these issues that early intervention services have been established. However, these are often targeted just at young people who are starting to experience psychosis – so that other people, such as those whose first experience of breakdown is in middle or later life, or younger people whose mental distress takes other forms, may still find that they are not picked up until their situation has reached crisis point.

Promoting more effective early detection can be achieved through:

- educating front-line professionals such as general practitioners and teachers to alert them to what may be early warning signs of mental distress;
- challenging stigma so that people experiencing the early stages of mental distress may feel less ashamed at coming forward;
- providing information about what mental health services are available and how to access them;
- having easily accessible direct intake services that can respond quickly;
- providing services in welcoming, non-stigmatising and 'user–friendly' environments – e.g. at home or in primary care centres.

Simple screening tools can be helpful in enabling people to distinguish between everyday unease and an emerging experience of mental distress. Many such tools developed within psychiatry can tend to be rather individually focused and can overemphasise biological 'symptoms' as against relationship or situational factors. Table 8.2 offers a screening tool which is adapted from the 10 QS screening tool for mental health (Falloon et al., 1996) to include more questions around social aspects of people's experience.

The use of such a tool fits well with principles of partnership working and empowerment. It does not set the practitioner up as the 'expert' who can perform some form of diagnosis upon the person. Instead it provides a set of prompts to start a dialogue which may lead to a shared understanding that the person may or may not be in need of more specialist support in relation to their mental health. A 'yes' to any question suggests the need for further exploration – but does not in itself determine that a person is experiencing mental distress. However, a number of 'yes' responses would start to give a strong indication that the person may be in need of help. Such a tool may be useful within a wider format of assessment and action planning (see Chapter 11).

Table 8.2 Screening tool for emerging signs of mental distress

		YES	NO
1	Do some of your thoughts or feelings seem to be running out of control?		
2	Have you any problems in relation to eating or sleeping?		
3	Have you passed the point where you can no longer cope with the everyday stresses and demands of your life?		
4	Any loss of energy or interests recently?		
5	Are you cutting yourself off from social situations that you would have been able to cope with before?		
6	Do you feel that people are checking up on you or are out to get you?		
7	Do you feel trapped and unable to change your situation?		
8	Have you been worrying more than usual about everyday problems?		
9	Do you sometimes feel compelled to harm or injure yourself?		
10	Have you had difficulty concentrating on reading or watching television – or following conversations?		
11	Do you ever feel that life is not worth living? Have you ever felt you would like to end it all?		
12	Do you find yourself acting in unusual ways – such as having to check things over and over again?		
13	Do you ever have attacks of panic or intense fear?		
14	Has anyone commented that your speech has become odd or difficult to understand?		
15	Do you ever hear people's voices when nobody seems to be around?		

Range of interventions and supports

Early intervention services provide a comprehensive range of thera-peutic responses that can help people to:

- hold on to or rebuild their resources of social capital, employ-ment and educational opportunities and their engagement within the life of their communities;
- address relationship issues;

- provide support to family and friends so that they can, in turn, provide a more effective network of emotional and practical support;
- work to change beliefs, feelings and ways of dealing with the world that have become dysfunctional.

Social and psychological supports and interventions are central to this approach (Power et al., 2007) – see Box 8.1.

Box 8.1 Non-medical services that may be part of an early intervention service

Individual counselling or psychotherapy.

Peer-group support for people with mental distress and/or for their carers and supporters.

Family therapy.

Education and information giving.

Onsite support to people to help them stay within their normal work or educational settings – or reintegrate back if they have had to have time off.

Support with maintaining or rebuilding social networks and social participation activities.

Support with housing and finance issues.

Such approaches may be combined with a low-dose medication regime (Power et al., 2007) or, more radically, with holding back on any introduction of medication to see if other supports and interventions prove sufficient to enable the person to manage their mental distress (Bola et al., 2009). Although the research evidence is far from clear, it is increasingly being recognised that medication can be a 'mixed blessing'. For some people, it can dampen down thinking and feeling in ways that can impair their ability to recognise or resolve the various personal and social issues that they may be facing. For others, medication may be helpful in managing certain problematic aspects of experience – such as hearing voices or feelings of depression – thereby enabling them to deal more effectively with other aspects of their situations. Where alternatives have been offered for people with early psychosis, a proportion do best with no medication, a proportion benefit from a low-dose medication regime, while some find they need moderate levels of medication for longer periods (Cullberg, 2006).

It is therefore crucial to move away from what has become custom and practice within many conventional mental health services: to rely on medication as the first response to problems of mental distress, and to see this as the preferred long-term solution to managing any difficulties. Medication cannot be a substitute for dealing with the social and psychological issues that may connect with people's mental distress – and using medication in this way may potentially make recovery harder for some people and induct them into to a long-term 'career' as a psychiatric patient. Instead, medication should be postponed or avoided if people can manage with other forms of support, or used selectively, on a short-term basis if possible, with close monitoring to allow it to be used at the lowest therapeutic dose.

Crisis resolution

In many instances, situations may have reached the point of crisis before any mental health services become involved. Not only may the person with mental distress be finding that their existing coping mechanisms are no longer working, but those around them may also be finding that they do not have the resources to cope and relationships may have become strained to breaking point. Even where early intervention services have been provided, the underlying dynamics of a situation may continue to impel it towards crisis – in some instances, things may have to get worse before they can start to get better.

Current approaches to crisis resolution build upon a long history of crisis intervention approaches (Caplan, 1965; Golan, 1986). A crisis presents a time of opportunity for change – and it may only be at the point of crisis when underlying issues come to the surface and there is sufficient urgency to resolve them. However, it is also a time of instability, risk and uncertainty – and change may not always be for the better. How we support people in a time of crisis can make the difference between laying the groundwork for a journey towards recovery, or inducting people into ongoing patterns of helplessness and dysfunction. Evaluations of crisis resolution services would indicate that around 80% of potential hospital admissions can be averted if intensive support is provided within community settings (Falloon and Fadden, 1993). Unfortunately, in many countries, a high proportion of current resources still tend to go into maintaining inpatient services that can be of dubious benefit in terms of enabling a positive resolution of mental health crises.

Crisis resolution approaches can provide the basis of innovative services that address the wider context of people's lives and maximise the potential for bringing about positive change. However, they represent a challenging and different way of working which goes against the grain of established medically dominated practice because they are 'based on the assumption that social factors are of central importance in understanding and managing ... crises' (Johnson and Needle, 2008, p. 6). Unfortunately, some mainstream services which are badged as 'crisis resolution' offer little more than home-based medical treatment and regular surveillance.

Sometimes set up as an alternative to mainstream services, and sometimes working in collaboration with statutory crisis resolution teams, a number of crisis houses and other services have been developed by people with direct experience of mental distress. These aim to 'normalise' rather than medicalise the experience of crisis, often helping people to retain their place within their social and family networks, and giving them the confidence to take a lead role in resolving their situation for themselves. It can be particularly empowering to receive support from staff who themselves have (and are willing to share) their lived experience of working through their own mental health crises (Dumont and Jones, 2007).

As with early intervention services, a number of experimental crisis services have been established where medication is not offered routinely – usually where community based crisis houses are available. The research evidence would suggest that certain forms of mental health crisis, such as psychosis, will tend to be self-limiting whether or not medication is offered – with both experimental and control groups showing similar levels of improvement in global psychopathology scores after six weeks (Mosher, 2004). This would suggest that, as longer-term (two-year) outcomes tended to be better for those who have had little or no medication, best practice should be to avoid or minimise the use of medication as the strategy of first choice.

What is a mental health crisis?

A crisis may either be the end-point of a long process of increasing instability and distress, or may be precipitated by some more immediate trigger which can break down the coping mechanisms of the person and their social environment (which may have been holding up reasonably well until then). Viewed systemically, mental health crises typically involve an interaction between two interlocking aspects:

1. a person's internal mental and emotional experience, which may
   - feel increasingly out of their control (*crisis of personal agency*);

- reflect a breakdown of active coping strategies and an escalation of defence mechanisms (*crisis of coping*);
- involve a disruption of their sense of self and familiar social identities (*crisis of identity and meaning*);

2. a person's social environment, which may be characterised by:
   - difficulty in sustaining social roles, duties and expectations (*crisis of social functioning*);
   - escalating tension within family or other relationships (*system crisis*);
   - disengagement from personal and social relationships (*crisis of connection with others*).

In some instances, a person's internal crisis may precede and contribute to a crisis in their social environment; in others, a crisis in the social environment may have arisen before, and may be seen as contributing to, their mental distress. In many instances, both 'inner' and 'outer' crises may develop simultaneously as part of interconnecting processes.

Typically, a crisis presents a relatively brief window of opportunity in which people may be open to accepting help and trying out new ways of relating to each other and dealing with their world – changes that may need to be supported and consolidated in the longer term if they are to hold. Most crises are resolved (for better or worse) within 4–6 weeks, and an investment of targeted support at this time may prove a very efficient use of resources.

In general terms, three possible types of outcome are possible:

1. 'Sticking-plaster' solutions that deal with some immediate presenting problems and allow the person and their social environment to revert to an uneasy version of the previous status quo – which is likely to remain unstable in the longer term if underlying issues have not been addressed.
2. Uncontrolled or catastrophic change in the absence of appropriate support. This may lead to a longer-term breakdown in mental functioning, a break up of relationships or social systems, or the imposition of even more oppressive or unliveable arrangements.
3. Getting (some of) the underlying issues out into the open and resolving them – allowing people to grow, recover and move on (Kanel, 2003).

Crisis resolution: principles and practice

The key principles that have been set out for crisis resolution teams fit well with the values and perspectives of a social approach:

- Services take a holistic approach, looking at all the factors involved in the crisis, including biological, psychological and social issues, and using a range of interventions to address these.
- The individual's social network has a powerful effect on the person's mental health, and treatment must directly address these significant social issues.
- Crisis staff should approach their work from a 'strengths' rather than an 'illness' model ...
- The approach should be one of collaborating with the user or their family by 'doing work with them' rather than 'doing work on them' so as to promote their 'ownership' of the crisis. (Sainsbury Centre for Mental Health, 2001, p. 3).

A number of different models of crisis intervention or crisis resolution have been proposed, each characterising it as a succession of stages (Golan, 1986; Roberts, 2000). Some are more focussed on the individual, their problems and their goals (Schnyder, 1997), while others focus more on their social context and, in particular what may have become problematic in their participation within family and other social systems (Bridgett and Polak, 2003). All approaches seek to describe a process which can support those involved in the crisis in a way which provides sufficient safety (so as to minimise the chance of negative or catastrophic outcomes), does not seek to impose any immediate 'sticking-plaster' solutions, but instead enables people to understand and resolve the issues that are contributing to their difficulties.

Typically, the process of crisis resolution involves the following stages.

Holding

It is important not to underestimate the levels of fear and distress that may be generated within a mental health crisis, both for the person and for those around them. This may lead to uncontrolled and not necessarily very coherent expressions of emotions, such as anger and sadness – sometimes located within discourses of blame (including self-blame) or victimisation. There may be a potential for this to spill over into violence – often not with any aggressive intent, but as a 'last-ditch' defence when other coping strategies are failing. Within such a volatile and unsupported environment, much may be expressed, but little may be heard, as people may be too preoccupied with their own feelings and perceptions. Whatever the emotional dynamics, it is important to receive and acknowledge people's feelings – listening and feeding back, but not commenting on or judging what people may be expressing at this stage. This may be surprisingly effective in calming situations and bringing people back into positions where they can more easily communicate and resolve issues.

Holding may involve practical steps to ensure immediate safety for all involved. One option may be to mobilise a network of allies and/or mental health staff to provide regular support in the person's own home – recognising that those family and friends who are acting as supporters may, in turn, require support in their own right. Alternatively, particularly if relationships with family or others have become fraught, a short stay in a crisis house or an adult placement may work better (where these are available), as long as connections with family and community can be maintained. Peer support from people with direct experience of mental distress can be particularly effective in providing hope and understanding.

Engaging

Building relationships with all those involved can be crucial in any process of crisis resolution. Engagement needs to take place in parallel with holding – together they enable people to feel a little safer. Core principles for engaging are:

- Do not take sides – form connections with both the person who is experiencing mental distress and with those around them and start finding out about each person's perspective.
- Convene a wider 'circle of support' – try to negotiate the inclusion of family, friends, neighbours and others who may be able to offer support and resources.
- Do not rescue or feel impelled to jump to instant solutions – a crucial skill is to be able just to *be* with people while they are in distress and enable them, at their pace, to start to work towards resolving whatever the distress is about.

Understanding

Once sufficient support is in place to take the edge off the crisis, but while there is still a sense of urgency and openness, it is time to work with those involved to make sense of what is going on. This window of opportunity may lead into a fuller process of comprehensive assessment and action planning (see Chapter 11).

This process may touch on difficult or sensitive issues, such as trauma or abuse – and it may be that the point of crisis is the first time that such issues may have started to come out into the open. This process may also highlight where family or other social systems are not functioning effectively and interventions may be helpful. There may need to be a balance between individual conversations where issues can be opened up, and family or group conversations where these can be explored and negotiated. Difficult issues can only be acknowledged and dealt with at a pace that is suitable for those involved. Before getting in too deep, it may be important to work on communication skills and to develop relationships of support and protection.

Resolving

The focus of crisis resolution is primarily on understanding and dealing with the *context* that may be contributing to someone's mental distress. There should be no expectation that a resolution of contextual and relationship issues will have an immediate impact on a person's mental distress – although in some instances this may subside surprisingly quickly once such issues are resolved or managed more effectively.

The role of the practitioner may be particularly important in facilitating an atmosphere in which all those involved feel sufficiently safe and supported to follow through and resolve outstanding issues. However, there can be a tendency, when the most acute phase of the crisis is over, for people to want to close down and avoid dealing with issues that may still feel difficult or painful:

> *Some members of my family, such as my mother and some friends, don't know how to react after a crisis. They seem scared to talk about it, almost as if they might be 'infected' by my problems or fearful that anything they might say might spark off another crisis. They avoid the subject altogether and instead talk of trivialities.* (Nadia, quoted in Thornicroft, 2006, p. 12)

A range of social approaches or interventions may prove helpful, including family therapy (Fadden, 2006; Gorell-Barnes, 1998) and social systems approaches (Bridgett and Polak, 2003; Polak, 1971). Such approaches may focus directly on resolving interpersonal difficulties, or may take a step back and work on developing skills and capacities so that people can resolve their difficulties for themselves. Either way, any resolution must come from, and be owned by, those who are involved in the situation.

Sustaining change

The changes and resolutions that emerge in the aftermath of a crisis may feel a little fragile – and there can be danger that support arrangements may fall apart, or new problems may knock relationships back to how they were. It can therefore be important to identify ways in which people can support each other in maintaining new ways of being with each other – and access external supports should they need them.

Longer-term success may depend on consolidating learning about *how* to resolve issues – developing 'capacities for independent problem resolution' (Healy, 2005, p. 126). Alongside this, it may be helpful to draw up relapse or crisis plans that build on what has been learned in order to specify the actions and supports that might be helpful if a crisis situation were to reoccur.

Social approaches, early intervention and crisis resolution

Both early intervention and crisis resolution approaches offer emerging ways of working which are genuinely holistic. They start with the 'bigger picture' of a person-in-context and do not inherently privilege a medicalisation of people's distress or a reduction of our field of view to one which focuses just on 'symptoms' or 'pathologies'. However, they only provide a conceptual 'shell' within which to organise therapeutic responses – one that needs to be filled by relevant theoretical understanding and collaborative practice approaches.

Currently, within many multidisciplinary teams, biomedical thinking and practice can be dominant – partly because a biomedical approach is more familiar and better understood. If this balance is to change, we need to deploy the research evidence and theoretical models that are explored in the preceding chapters in order to identify the particular social and personal issues that may be contributing to a person's mental distress and how these may be resolved – with a particular focus on what may be the strengths and resources that could be mobilised in order to change their situation. Effective strategies for early intervention and crisis resolution involve working, not just with the individual, but also with family, social networks and the wider community.

Summary of key points

- Both early intervention and crisis resolution approaches have the potential to minimise the loss of social roles and connections and maximise the possibility of recovery.
- Many (but not all) people achieve best outcomes with no medication or low-dose medication regimes.
- Models of early intervention focus on
  - mental health awareness;
  - early detection;
  - an integrated range of interventions and supports to address personal issues and maximise social engagement.
- A crisis resolution approach sees a crisis as an opportunity to resolve the social and interpersonal issues that may be contributing to a person's distress.
- It comprises a series of stages:
  - holding;
  - engaging;
  - understanding;
  - resolving;
  - sustaining change;

  and it involves working with a person *and* their family and social support systems.

Further reading

Early intervention:

Birchwood, M., Fowler, D., & Jackson, C. (eds) (2002). *Early Intervention in Psychosis*. Chichester: Wiley.

French, P., Smith, J., Shiers, D., Reed, M., & Rayne, M. (2010). *Promoting Recovery in Early Psychosis*. Oxford: Blackwell.

Crisis resolution:

Johnson, S., Needle, J., Bindman, J., & Thornicroft, G. (eds) (2008). *Crisis Resolution and Home Treatment in Mental Health*. Cambridge: Cambridge University Press.

User-run and other alternative service models:

Stastny, P., & Lehmann, P. (eds) (2007). *Alternatives Beyond Psychiatry*. Berlin: Peter Lehmann.

9 | Recovery and social participation

The current concept of 'recovery' has emerged from the service user movement and challenges much of conventional thinking and practice in mental health (Social Care Institute for Excellence et al., 2007) – although there are concerns that it runs the danger of being colonised by professionally based definitions and thereby losing its radical edge. In this chapter, I will explore what 'recovery' means and what are its implications for socially oriented practice.

An important component of recovery can be re-engaging within mainstream social life (Mezzina et al., 2006) – but, within many mental health services, work to support social inclusion and relationship building can often be insufficiently prioritised. In order to redress this, it may be helpful for social workers to see one of their key roles in supporting recovery-oriented practice as being to champion social inclusion within multi-disciplinary teams:

What is recovery?

Recovery is not primarily about becoming 'symptom-free', but may be defined in social, personal and sometimes spiritual terms as *'the aspiration … to live, work and love in a community in which one makes a significant contribution'* (Deegan, 1988, p. 15). It is seen as a *journey*, not an *end-state*, and it may involve:

- finding meaning and purpose in life;
- achieving full citizenship and (re)establishing social connections;
- discovering positive personal and social identities;
- reclaiming personal efficacy and control over one's life;
- having strategies for managing any ongoing difficulties.

There can be different emphases depending on one's cultural context, sometimes with more of a focus on a personal journey of self-discovery within individualised Western cultures, and a focus on re-establishing one's place in family and community, and achieving spiritual balance and harmony, within more collective or spiritually based cultures. For some people, recovery may mean exiting from mental health services, either permanently or for much of the time. For others, it may mean continuing to receive ongoing forms of medical, personal or social support that enable them to get on with their lives.

This turns on its head the conventional assumption that people have to 'get better' first before they can consider reintegrating back into active citizenship – and that 'getting better' can only be achieved through passive acquiescence to medical treatment. Instead, the recovery movement suggests that people need to take charge of reclaiming a lifestyle that is meaningful to them, and take an active role in dealing with their voices, moods, self-harming behaviours or other manifestations of their mental distress. Although not the primary intention, it is often through focusing on 'getting a life' that people may also find that their 'symptoms' abate or go away altogether.

The evidence from longitudinal studies lends support to this perspective. Contrary to the impression given out by many services that serious mental 'illness' is a long-term and deteriorating condition, the majority of people do recover over time (Harding et al., 1987; Warner, 1994) – either finding that their 'symptoms' no longer interfere with their life (social recovery), or achieving a full remission of distress experiences.

Perhaps surprisingly, there is no evidence that the introduction of new medical treatments over the last century has had any positive impact on recovery rates. Instead, in Western countries, both social recovery rates and full remission of 'symptoms' have correlated closely with economic cycles (Warner, 1994). This would suggest that, when it is easier for people with mental distress to re-engage with work (and the social statuses that this can provide), this can enable them to recover. Other research confirms that people with serious 'mental illness' who are supported back into employment do better than controls in terms of both reduction in social disability *and* remission of 'symptoms' (Burns et al., 2009). Interestingly, cross-cultural comparisons show that some more traditional societies have recovery rates that are twice as high as in the West – perhaps where there is less stigmatisation of mental distress and a higher expectation that people will slot back into valued social roles in family life or in the workforce (Warner, 1994).

Taken together, this evidence supports the view that it is primarily what people do with their life that determines their recovery – and what they are able to do depends on the social opportunities and supports that are (or are not) available to them.

Recovery as empowerment

Central to recovery is reclaiming one's personal efficacy and control over one's life (Chamberlin, 1997; Coleman, 1999a; Deegan, 1997). One cannot be empowered by others – but one can be given opportunities to claim power for oneself, both individually and in collaboration with others. The matrix of power relations developed in Chapter 4 may help to map one's current situation and identify productive directions of change – in particular, avoiding locking horns and competing with others in an imagined 'zero-sum game' and instead looking more laterally at how to construct effective forms of *co-operative* and *protective* power.

Finding a way out of disability and powerlessness can be crucial if one is to shed 'the role of victim in exchange for a new attitude of personal responsibility and self-efficacy' (Young and Ensing, 1999, p. 224):

> 'Giving up being a schizophrenic is not an easy thing to do, for it means taking back responsibility for yourself, it means that you can no longer blame your illness for your actions … It means that you stop being a victim of your experience and start being the owner of your experience.' (Coleman, 1999b, pp. 160–1)

In this way, recovery involves changing one's power relationship with one's distress experiences. The evidence indicates that disempowerment in one's dealings with one's external world can spill over into feeling powerless in relation to aspects of one's internal world – such as feeling dominated by one's voices (Birchwood et al., 2000). This suggests a very different approach to working with voices: instead of using medication or other means to try to quieten the voices, it may be more productive to work on enhancing people's personal efficacy so that they can resist any inappropriate commands, or dispute (or shrug off) any disparaging comments (Romme and Escher, 2000). Narrative and dialogue approaches can give people the opportunity to name, externalise and talk to problematic 'symptoms' – whether they be emotional states, internal voices or irrational beliefs – and, by talking with them, start to 'cut them down to size', no longer giving them the power to take over and define their whole persona (Coleman and Smith, 1997; Corstens et al., 2009; White and Epston, 1990).

Working to support recovery

Recovery is not something that can be 'done to' a person by well-meaning practitioners (or friends or family): it is the person's own journey that starts when they are ready to start and proceeds at their pace. However, the values, attitudes and practices of those around can be crucial in enabling or disabling this process (see Chapter 1):

> *'It's very hard if you find other people are making decisions about your life and that they think they know best.'* (Scottish Recovery Network, 2006 p. 27)

The social and the personal aspects of a recovery journey interconnect and potentially reinforce one another: both can be necessary if someone is to move forward. Positive social experiences and statuses help to restore self-esteem and social participation can provide contexts for developing personal efficacy or trying out new ways of relating. (Re)-establishing social and family connections – and perhaps taking on some limited responsibilities, such as voluntary work or informal caring – can be important in finding meaning in one's new situation. Conversely, exploring and resolving some of the personal (and interpersonal) issues that may be holding one back can give one more energy for social involvement – and help one to choose the sorts of social involvement that one would like.

Practitioners can play an important role in supporting and enabling (but not directing) these processes of experimentation, discovery and change – and in helping people to reflect on and learn from their experiences. They can be a vital 'holder of hope', particularly when progress seems difficult or uncertain (Glover, 2003). It can be important to reassure people that setbacks are almost inevitably part of a process that will ultimately lead to recovery. Some setbacks may feel as if one is returning to square one, temporarily revisiting a place of anguish or disconnection. However, it is likely that one's progress so far will give one additional resources with which to deal with the setback, and 'bottoming out' may be rather quicker than the first time around. Reflecting on setbacks can be an important source of learning – perhaps developing a clearer awareness of issues not yet resolved, or discovering what may be the most effective coping strategies in the face of particular difficulties.

Setting the context for recovery: social acceptance and social opportunities

Although social engagement is crucial to recovery, there can still be an over-emphasis on approaching this from the perspective of the individual, rather than also working at a community level to develop a social context of acceptance and opportunity into which people can be enabled to recover. Without this, effort and resources ploughed into individualised services may achieve only limited results, given the evidence that social context that can have such a major impact on recovery rates.

Progress has been made in a number of countries in promoting mental health awareness and anti-stigma campaigns in order to reduce barriers to social acceptance – and the potential impact of these can be reinforced by disability and equalities legislation which may have some 'teeth' in terms of forcing organisations and structures to start to make reasonable adjustments in order to be inclusive of people with mental health difficulties. The evidence would suggest that stigmatising attitudes and representations are changed most effectively through personal encounters (Kolodziej and Johnson, 1996) – and so it is locally based anti-stigma work carried out by people with direct experience of mental distress that can be most effective in breaking down barriers between 'us' and 'them' (Glasgow Anti-Stigma Partnership, 2007).

Alongside work to promote social acceptance, there can be a need for more practical community level initiatives to develop social capital and opportunities for paid and voluntary work. It can be important to engage directly with employers and providers of education, housing and other services to put in support systems that will work for both 'sides' should any difficulties arise as people with mental distress take up mainstream opportunities. Often providers may fear that the person with mental distress is going to be abandoned by support services and that their organisation may be left to deal with a situation that is beyond their understanding or capability. Successful initiatives are often based on contractual arrangements that may offer a tapering programme of support initially, followed up by arms-length monitoring and rapid response should any problems emerge (Carling, 1995; Drake et al., 1996).

Affirmative personal relationships

Research suggests that personal relationships are often the decisive factor in people's recovery journeys, either being 'conducive or detrimental to recovery' (Schon et al., 2009, p. 345). It is these that can provide the linchpin of support and recognition that enables people to move forward in both the personal and social aspects of their recovery journeys. A mental health crisis can highlight all too dramatically who one's friends really are; people who may have previously been somewhat overlooked may emerge as stalwarts of reliability, while relationships with best friends may crumble or be revealed as one-sided or abusive.

For many people, particularly valuable support can come from peer relationships with others who have direct experience of mental distress (Clay et al., 2005). These can provide a special form of acceptance and understanding, grounded in a commonality of experience. Such relationships can arise through spontaneous friendships that may be made through meeting people in hospital or other mental health services. In a less accidental way, they may arise through joining self-help or mutual support groups, or connecting with people who have taken on more formal roles as support workers, advocates or 'buddies'.

Such small-scale experiences of *co-operative* power have often been identified as crucial turning points in people's recovery journeys. Whether they are with friends, family, peers or professionals, research shows that the sorts of personal relationships that promote recovery are those that respect and value one as a unique person, encourage the use of one's 'own resources and capacities', and enable the emergence of one's personal efficacy through 'concrete experiences of being able to exert influence over one's own life circumstances' (Schon et al., 2009, p. 345).

Tig's story (Davies, 2006) provides a first-hand account of how such affirmative relationships may come about and the impact that they can have. Following a period of 'going nowhere', with repeated hospital admissions, a severe problem with eating, and voices that demanded that she harmed herself, she met a woman called Dee who ran the café for patients and visitors in the hospital:

> *'Dee didn't just serve coffee, she served people. She talked, she shared, she asked, she listened, she cried, she laughed, she spoke the truth as she saw it, she hugged when appropriate, kept her distance when it was right to do so. She joined people to communicate, she took no crap from people, she sought and found understanding of difference – oh, and she made a great mug of coffee!'*

It was in Dee's café that Tig encountered a new welfare rights worker called Dave, and she, Dee and Dave drank coffee together. It was within this context that Dave asked her what *she* thought would help her to get well again. This had a surprisingly profound impact on her:

'I was blown away – no one had asked me before and I had always been led to believe that the pills, the nurses and the psychiatrists had the answers. After all, they had written me a care plan! … Feeling I had nothing to lose, I told Dave and Dee the threads of a dream I had known before. I wanted to be well, I wanted relationships with my family and friends back, I wanted to go home to my flat, and I wanted to work. At the end of this talk I ate and, equally important, "enjoyed" toast and jam and a full mug of chocolate milkshake. At that point I hadn't eaten more than one digestive biscuit and half a glass of milk a day for over three months! I also smiled. And that felt great. "Hope" had finally returned.'

This was a turning point as a result of which she started to re-establish relationships with family and friends, and then to make a tentative start as a welfare rights volunteer at the hospital.

This story offers some key messages to practitioners and services:

1. The human encounter can be more important than any technical skill or treatment protocol in terms of bringing about positive change.
2. A vital but often underrated role for mental health services is to create contexts in which collaborative encounters can take place and affirmative relationships develop.
3. It is important for many people to be able to give as well as to receive (albeit to a limited extent) – and emergent relationships of *co-operative* power may be crucial for a person in regaining their sense of personal efficacy.

The path to recovery

In understanding the nature of a recovery journey, it is important that we consider what it is that a person may need to recover from. This may include, not just the distress experience itself, but also:

- the trauma, loss and social dislocation that may have resulted from it (see Chapter 7);
- the potentially 'spirit-breaking' impact of oppressive service interventions on their already fragile sense of self (Deegan, 1989);
- conflictual, unequal or oppressive personal relationships;
- the legacy of past traumas and adverse life experiences;
- the ongoing impact of discrimination, poverty and disadvantage.

While every person's journey is unique, analyses of people's narratives have identified many common themes and processes, including acceptance, affirmative and supportive relationships, finding meaning in one's experience and dealing with unresolved personal or social issues. Such themes may be seen in the excerpt from a recovery narrative reproduced in Box 9.1.

Box 9.1   Excerpt from 'There is more to me than my mental health'

'I became aware that I had a real problem that I couldn't make sense of and that I didn't feel I had anyone to confide in. My hallucinations and paranoia were leading me to become very scared and I trusted no one ...

This social worker recognised a troubled person, but also my potential, and provided me with the space and continuity to actually build up a relationship. I was still [hearing voices] and was very depressed. I was still in and out of hospital and various supported accommodation. In one hostel I began to challenge myself, my situation and how I might gain control over my experiences and life. I kept asking myself, 'Is this it? Is this how life is going to be for me?' ...

My relationship over this time with my social worker has been the key thing for me. I began to realise that there were people who believed that there was more to me than my mental health ... The emotional support I received helped and encouraged me to understand myself and my experiences in the context of everyday life ...

One of the major things I struggled with was this thing called 'insight' ... How could my reality be anything other than real? I tried to sort through things with a combination of reading, talking, and linking past life experiences to present distorted reality. However, understanding didn't come easily and, at times, I felt it would be easier to accept and stay in my distorted reality.

Challenging my thoughts and experiences was difficult, especially as I didn't quite believe that it was the right thing to do. Thankfully the pay-off has been worth it. I am extremely grateful to those who gave me the space to explore myself in the way I did. For me it was much more valuable than some form of formal interaction/therapy. I needed to feel that I was a whole person rather than a bunch of symptoms that had to be managed or controlled.'

Source: Scottish Recovery Network, 2006, pp. 25–7. Reproduced with permission.

Journeys progress through various steps (see Figure 9.1), but not necessarily in a very linear fashion – and many people may find that they need to go back to a previous stage before they can go forward again (Ralph et al., 1999). Fundamental to recovery is rediscovering personal efficacy – which involves the right to take risks, make mistakes and learn from these experiences. People may need to 'grope in the dark' to find their identities and place in the world in much the same way as negotiating their first transition into adulthood. For most people, recovery involves a twin-track approach of increasing (if initially tentative) social engagement alongside a more personal journey of awareness and change. Factors that may support recovery include aspects of people's *resilience* that may still be intact, *affirmative personal relationships* and a social context that provides *acceptance* and *opportunities*.

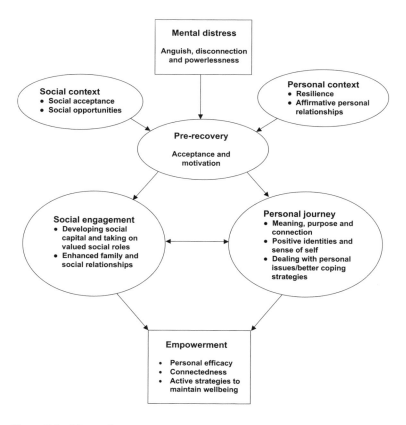

Figure 9.1   The path to recovery

Pre-recovery: acceptance and motivation

In some ways, the first step is the hardest, both to take and to understand how others can best facilitate this. While a person is in the grip of an episode of mental distress, they can feel impelled by forces that are outside their control that take them towards ever more extreme experiences until they hit some form of 'rock bottom' of anguish or disconnection (Ralph et al., 1999). It is a slide that can be hard to arrest, as it can feel as though they are being irrevocably drawn to a place that they have to visit (and sometimes revisit) before recovery can be possible. People recount how, although such a place may have been incredibly painful or disturbing, it could ultimately be life-changing in a positive way – perhaps forcing them to acknowledge something which needed to be addressed.

> 'Though distressing and disabling, I have always thought of my symptoms as "allies"' even when things are most difficult. The symptoms, which arose from systematic and prolonged childhood trauma, gave me "clues"– like a kind of road map – towards recovery, alongside staying involved with what is good in my life.' ('Paving my own way' in Scottish Recovery Network, 2006, p. 29)

Some people seem to bottom out of such experiences of their own accord, putting them in a place where they may begin their recovery journey. This may involve giving up coping strategies that are not working and 'facing the fear' of what may come next. However, others seem to get stuck at or around rock bottom for some time – in a state in which they may feel disconnected both from aspects of themselves and from their social (and even physical) environment. People may feel overwhelmed by the intensity of their mental distress, or demoralised by it (Bradshaw et al., 2007).

Paradoxically, one cannot start having realistic hopes for the future – and working towards these – until one has accepted where one is in the present: 'Acceptance means seeing and acknowledging all the various aspects of oneself without devaluing oneself' (Spaniol and Gagne, 1997, p. 75). It involves moving beyond the various strategies of denial that may have been part of one's coping mechanisms – and recognising that it is highly unlikely that one will be able to go back to where one was before the episode of mental distress. It also involves acknowledging that one's distress experiences are part of who one is and are likely to remain so, at least for the time being – and that one may need the help and support of others in order to move forward. What it does not mean is that one has to accept that one has an 'illness'. Nor does it mean – although this can be hard to avoid – that one has to buy in to the social stigmatisation that may attach to such experiences.

Accepting ourselves and our distress can be much easier if those around us are already accepting of us, both in terms of our strengths and potential *and* our distress experiences:

> '*Ros was the first person who didn't recoil in disgust or be angry, negative or distressed about my need to self-injure. She understood that was where I was at in my life and she accepted me whether I harmed or didn't harm. I didn't have to hide it, justify it, or make bargains or promises I couldn't keep ... For the first time I had some control over my circumstances.*' (Pembroke, 2009, p. 233)

For some people, medication may serve to improve their level of contact with aspects of reality and hence their ability to move on from their experience. For others, the very same medication may act as a long-term insulator, keeping them from ever getting in touch with what their distress is about and maintaining them in a form of suspended animation that may go on for many years. The routine use of medication may be unhelpful and it should only be used where people experience particular benefits – and, where possible, on a short-term and low-dose basis. Where someone seems to have become stuck in their distress, a conventional response can be to increase their medication in an attempt to control their 'symptoms'. However, it may be more helpful to try the opposite and accept that, in the short term, their distress may become more acute – but this may be necessary if they are to be able to work through to the other side.

Where people have become stuck in profound distress experiences, any actions which assist them to re-establish contact with aspects of self and with other people (or just with their physical surroundings) can be important. This may involve spending time with people in very low-key ways, perhaps just sitting with them and saying very little, or joining with them in undertaking very simple tasks such as going for a walk together. It may also be helpful to acknowledge and reflect back to people their words or expressions so as to assist them to be more aware of themselves (Prouty et al., 2002).

The start of a recovery journey involves discovering motivation – the first glimmerings of returning personal efficacy. Supporting this process may involve responding to any initiative that people may make – however small and tentative this may be. Gentle forms of challenge may also be important, perhaps suggesting to people that they may be underrating their capabilities or potentials:

> *'My [care co-ordinator] never gave up her faith in my abilities to change my life. She saw that I was a fighter. But she challenged my actions, giving honest information about the consequences.'*
> (Williams, 2009, p. 219)

Practitioners or family members may not always be the best people to make such challenges – which may easily be interpreted as 'nagging' or 'telling off' – whereas they may be received more constructively if they come from peers who have their own lived experience of distress. *Co-operative* rather than *protective* forms of power can be the most effective means of bringing about change.

Finding meaning, purpose and connection

Many people express a strong desire to make sense of their distress experiences (and how these fit with the rest of their life experience) in order to take some control over what is actually happening to them. It is this that may start to give them a sense of direction or purpose in life. While the process of finding meaning and developing understanding may take place in the context of a therapeutic relationship with a professional helper, this may equally well take place within everyday friendships or within mutual support groups such as the Hearing Voices Network – and it is important that alternatives are available to people.

The biomedical model may be less than helpful in providing a framework of meaning as it can situate people as helpless victims of a disease process that is outside their control, having to wait passively until 'experts' can make them better. However, this is not necessarily so, and people may become experts on their mental state, learning which medications are helpful and what dosage works best – and perhaps taking on responsibility for varying their own medication within defined limits.

For many people, the most helpful frameworks of meaning are ones which enable them to make connections between their internal and external worlds (Geekie, 2004; Ridge and Ziebland, 2006). The frameworks explored in Chapters 2 to 7 may provide helpful pointers (for example in making connections with experiences of trauma or discrimination) – but it is for people themselves to come up with ways of understanding that make sense to them.

Such frameworks may be idiosyncratic and may relate to their cultural or religious background. They may sometimes appear bizarre to professional helpers – but experience suggests that ideas that are developed and owned by people themselves are more successful in enabling recovery than any 'insights' that may be imposed by well-meaning practitioners.

The content of many 'symptoms' may give clues as to what the distress is about: they may provide indirect or metaphoric expressions of unresolved issues. For example, in understanding voice-hearing experiences, it may be important to explore who the voices may represent, the content of what they are saying and how this may relate to people's lives (Coleman and Smith, 1997). By accepting and taking voices seriously, many people are able to change their relationship with their more problematic voices so that they are less distressing, intrusive or overbearing – or learn from their voices what may be underlying issues that they may need to resolve.

Positive identities and sense of self

For many people, a mental health crisis dislocates and brings into question their sense or who they are, so that a 'quest for identity' can become 'the driving force behind perception, interpretation and decision throughout the early stages of recovery' (Pettie and Triolo, 1999, p. 256). Reconstructing a sense of self – and reclaiming personal agency – can be crucial for recovery. This may involve creating a new 'coherent life narrative' (Roe and Davidson, 2005) that incorporates past experience and current circumstances, and also the meanings and understandings that may emerge as people start to 'story' their distress experiences. Rebuilding self esteem may involve re-evaluating experiences of abuse or discrimination within new 'survivor' narratives that move beyond guilt and self-blame – and allow people to see what happened as unjust and an abuse of power:

> *'I have realised that I am recovering from the discrimination as much as I am recovering from the mental health problems.'* (service user, quoted in Scottish Recovery Network, 2008)

What can be particularly helpful in supporting people in rebuilding positive self-identities is to relate to them on the basis of their strengths rather than their (temporary) deficits: focusing on their competence, abilities and courage, and enabling them to make contact with, and build upon, their resilience (Saleeby, 2006).

Such processes of rebuilding can easily be undermined by the insidious internalisation of stigma – so a helpful focus can be on 'stigma resistance' (Sibitz et al., 2009). This can be enabled by social relationships that reinforce ordinary life and 'whole person' identities – and a refusal to take on the identity of 'patient' through keeping the main focus of one's life outside the mental health system. For some people, successful stigma resistance may also involve refusing to accept one's medical diagnosis (Lysaker et al., 2009) – which may unfortunately bring one into conflict with some mental health services.

Dealing with personal issues and finding better coping strategies

Some people find it helpful to work alongside a professional helper in relation to the more personal aspects of their therapeutic journey:

> 'I slowly started to shift and open up my heart to change ... I started to talk about my feelings, my life and fears ... This went further back and deeper than outward signs of distress ... I wasn't allowed to blame 'illness' for my feelings, but was expected to look at what was going on. I objected to the term "learnt behaviour" but over time could see how I'd laid down ways of coping in my formative years.' (Williams, 2009, p. 219)

Others may prefer to work things out in their own ways, perhaps with the support of key friends or family members – as in the narrative presented in Box 9.1.

Although some therapeutic approaches (such as cognitive behavioural therapy) are easier to evaluate than others, there is little overall evidence that any particular approach is necessarily more effective than any other – and there is a danger that sticking rigidly to specific 'evidence-based' therapeutic protocols may result in missing the complexity of connections between the personal and the social, or the creativity of people's own insights and solutions.

Social capital and valued social roles

In parallel with (and interacting with) one's personal journey is the process of re-establishing one's 'place in the world' (Bradshaw et al., 2007) – which may involve some combination of resuming social roles and reactivating social networks that were part of one's former social world, and developing new social connections. It is only within such social contexts that one can start to reconstruct one's sense of self and social identities (Mezzina et al., 2006).

As we saw in Chapter 7, the social consequences of mental distress may involve losing, temporarily or permanently, much of one's access to social capital and the world of work. Without rebuilding some of this, recovery may not be possible. Unfortunately, being sucked into the mental health system can easily make temporary losses permanent and militate against accessing new forms of social capital and employment within the mainstream social world. Therefore any strategies that minimise this disruption may be crucial to recovery – such as managing crises at home or in locally based crisis houses, and having support in resuming many of one's former involvements, perhaps with some renegotiation and adjustment.

However, where roles may have been stressful and relationships fraught, there may be very good reasons not to go back to the old. Experiences of mental distress can provide opportunities for reappraisal of one's lifestyles and involvements – and one may wish for support in accessing new social or employment opportunities. Achieving this may involve intermediate steps such as further education or retraining, volunteering or taking up a new hobby or recreational activity.

Working to develop social capital requires a twin-track approach that focuses both on structural and cognitive aspects. As was discussed earlier, community-based interventions may be important to develop concrete opportunities for networking, training and occupation within mainstream social settings. Alongside this, personal coaching may be helpful in enabling people to discover their vision of where they are going, and providing encouragement and practical support along the way. It may also be useful for people to have a 'buddy' to accompany them when they first start to 'dip their toes into the water' of new and challenging social situations. Cognitive therapies may be useful in challenging negative (and self-excluding) messages that people may have internalised as to their relationship to, and place within, the social world around them – and replacing these with more constructive beliefs about self and others that may underpin the development of cognitive social capital.

For those who wish to enter mainstream employment, recent approaches have overturned conventional thinking. Instead of being expected to achieve a higher level of functioning through undertaking programmes of vocational rehabilitation *before* one could be considered ready to start an 'open' work placement, it has now been shown that entering the world of work can itself play a part in one's recovery journey. Even for people with higher levels of functional disability, immersion within in a mainstream work environment can result in higher success rates – not just in terms of employment outcomes, but also in relation to wider measures of social functioning and remission of symptoms (Burns et al., 2009). Key to this approach (termed Individual Placement and Support) is offering support both to people *and* their employers as they ease themselves back into the world of work – enabling people to take on an active and socially engaged identity as an employee, instead of an exclusionary identity such as 'mental patient' (Borg and Kristiansen, 2008).

Working with family and social systems

Too much of a focus on the individual and their care or treatment can mean that relationship issues – and the concerns of those around them – may not be identified or addressed:

> 'They don't ask me what I need. All of the things that I have said I would have found helpful, I have been told are not available. I'd like two things: family intervention and mediation.' (carer, quoted in Repper et al., 2008, p. 427)

In Chapter 6, we explored how certain dynamics and communication patterns can sometimes impact adversely on people's mental health. Over and above this, mental health crises can affect relationships with significant others, leaving people unsure as to how best to provide support – and also with their own fears and concerns as to how all this may affect them. Recovery may need to be a process of change that involves all those who are part of a person's situation.

The approach of social systems intervention, pioneered by Paul Polak (Bridgett and Polak, 2003; Polak, 1971), and systemic approaches to family therapy (Gorell-Barnes, 1998) provide frameworks for making relationship systems, rather than the person's inner world, the primary locus for change. All system members may be supported in bringing issues out into the open so that they can be resolved:

> 'I think it is important to have a recovery process for carers – do any of us have the life we want? ... It's good to think about recovery as ... a process that applies to everyone.' (carer, quoted in Scottish Recovery Network, 2009, p. 30)

Resolution of issues may involve some renegotiation of system rules, or of people's positioning relative to one another. Through a focus on relationships, it may become possible to mobilise more effective forms of *co-operative* and *protective* power – and hence to enhance the capacity of the system to support the recovery of everyone within it. Alongside this, the resolution of identified problems may involve interventions with wider systems such as housing, employment or local community networks.

There are now well-developed ways of working on communication issues – such as Behavioural Family Therapy – which can enable people to clarify and renegotiate aspirations, concerns and expectations within an atmosphere of support and mutual engagement (Fadden, 2006). A key outcome from such a constructive problem-solving approach can be to *'permit the development of independence in someone who may need to relearn it'* (carer, quoted in Scottish Recovery Network, 2009, p. 18).

Meta-analyses of family interventions indicate that these can be effective in bringing about recovery outcomes, as long as the support is sustained over a substantial period of time (over nine months). No particular model seems to work best overall – and different approaches seem to suit particular families (Glynn et al., 2006). Characteristics of effective family support programmes include:

- instilling hope for the future;
- showing concern and empathy to all family members;
- avoiding blaming the family or pathologising their efforts to cope;
- fostering the development of *all* family members;
- decreasing stress;
- strengthening communication and problem solving abilities;
- encouraging family members to develop social supports outside their family network;
- taking a long-term perspective (ibid., p. 454).

However, some family approaches are still embedded in an 'educating families to cope with a long term illness' paradigm, and fail sufficiently to respect 'the context of the family as *crucial to recovery* and incorporate assessment processes which seek to document the strengths and resilience of the family' (Addington et al., 2001, p. 272).

A focus on communication issues and learning more effective communication skills can have quite far-reaching results in terms of shifting the relative positioning of (and power relations between) family or group members. In particular, it can offer possibilities for previously marginalised people (children and overburdened carers as well as people with mental distress) to be heard and taken seriously – and thereby start to reclaim their efficacy and identities within family or group interactions.

Empowerment, connection and active strategies to maintain wellbeing

Through processes of personal struggle and social engagement, many people will, to a greater or lesser extent, reclaim their ability to take control over their lives. This may involve both rediscovering personal efficacy (Mancini, 2007) and mobilising *power together* through social relationships and participation in community life (Nelson et al., 2001a). In addition, it may involve developing specific strategies by which to take active control over maintaining one's wellbeing – and perhaps also having ways of managing certain ongoing 'symptoms' of mental distress:

> 'I'm in control now. I used to hear voices from the TV, the voices would talk to me and tell me to do things ... I used to do what they told me to do, but now ... I still hear them, but I've learned not to listen to them ... I'm back in reality now ... I learned to deal with it myself.' (David, quoted in Warren, 2003, pp. 37–8)

For some, these strategies may involve managing one's life independently of services – perhaps being vigilant for potential sources of stress that might trigger some form of relapse, and having recourse to a repertoire of active coping strategies should they be needed. For Esso Leete, this entailed quite a self-disciplined programme of:

1. *'recognising when I am feeling stressed, which is harder than it may sound;*
2. *identifying the stressor;*
3. *remembering from past experience what action helped in the same situation or a similar one; and*
4. *taking that action as quickly as possible after I have identified the source of the stress.'* (Leete, 1989, quoted in Repper and Perkins, 2003, p. 115)

Such active coping strategies may be consciously chosen and controlled – and may be very different from former response patterns or defence mechanisms that might still cause one to relapse into mental distress.

For other people, strategies for maintaining wellbeing may involve being able to rely on the support of family and friends – or organising ongoing forms of support (as and when needed), perhaps through having control of one's personal budget. People may find it helpful to use an approach such as Wellness Recovery Action Planning (see Chapter 11) for a more focused exploration of what works for them and to devise specific plans and strategies for staying well. Particularly for people who may experience psychosis, the secret may be to maintain a comfortable level of social engagement but have the option of already planned 'escape routes' if stresses (or general levels of stimulation) become too great at any point in time.

Summary of key points

- Recovery is a journey that involves:
  - finding meaning and purpose in life;
  - achieving full citizenship and (re)establishing social connections;
  - discovering positive personal and social identities;
  - reclaiming personal efficacy and control over one's life;
  - having strategies for managing any ongoing difficulties.
- Work with families, networks and communities is crucial if people are to have the opportunity to recover.
- The most important factor in enabling recovery is having affirmative personal and social relationships.
- Enabling recovery involves a 'twin-track' approach, enabling social engagement and supporting people as they work through the more personal aspects of their recovery journeys and find more effective coping strategies.

Further reading

Coleman, R. (1999) *Recovery? An Alien Concept.* Gloucester: Handsell.

Repper, J., & Perkins, R. (2003). *Social Inclusion and recovery.* London: Baillière Tindall.

Roberts, G. (ed.) (2006) *Enabling Recovery.* London: Gaskell.

Saleebey, D. (2006) *The Strengths Perspective in Social Work Practice (4th ed.).* New York: Allyn & Bacon.

Scottish Recovery Network (2009) *Carers and Supporting Recovery.* www.scottishrecovery.net/view-document/236

Slade, M. (2009) *Personal Recovery and Mental Illness: A Guide for Mental Health Professionals.* Cambridge: Cambridge University Press.

In addition there is a range of useful material, including survivor narratives, available via the Scottish Recovery Network website www.scottishrecovery.net

10 | Risk taking and safeguarding

One of the most contentious areas of mental health practice is around issues of risk. In this chapter, I will review how risk may be understood and the conclusions for practice that may be drawn from research. On the basis of this, I will then look at what may be more empowering approaches to risk taking and safeguarding. For some people, in some situations, compulsory intervention may be the only option – but this can be at some cost to the person who is detained and to their social relationships. I will therefore explore how the use of compulsion, and its adverse impact, may be minimised.

Discourses of risk

Over recent years, there has been a growing social concern about issues of risk in economically advanced societies (Beck, 1992). Perhaps due to more rapid social change and mobility, people seem to have a greater need to hold on to a sense of control and certainty in their lives. In turn, this has led to a particular fixation with the out-of-control behaviour *of 'others'* and the risk it may pose to *'us'*. Fear of crime has increased even when the actual incidence of crime has diminished, and moral panics have escalated around constructions of dangerous 'others' such as paedophiles or the 'mentally ill' – with isolated incidents, such as the unprovoked killing of Jonathan Zito by Christopher Clunis, being accorded untoward significance.

Theoretically, this links to the idea of how more general concerns or unease may become crystallised as a 'risk object' that starts to appear and be referred to in media representations, policy discussions and everyday conversations (Hilgartner, 1992). This 'object' becomes linked to the possibility of harm and to definitions of who is responsible for doing something about it, and who can be blamed if anything goes wrong (Douglas, 1992). Whereas the old asylums acted as a visible and symbolic guarantor that risk was being contained (and 'we' were being protected from 'them'), moves towards community care created uncertainties which began to take on a momentum of their own (Warner, 2007). Picking up on the news stories from isolated homicide enquiries, where a common thread seemed to be that no one was properly in charge of people's care, a vision began to emerge across the British press of the 'dangerous schizophrenic' loose upon the streets (Wilkinson, 1998). This vision was then echoed in the government's framing of the case for the reform of the Mental Health Act in England.

The emergence of the 'mentally ill' as a risk object has no basis in any actual increase in risk, despite the fact that the funding and quality of community care services have not always lived up to expectations. Internationally, studies show no increase in total rates of homicide committed by people with serious mental distress during the shift from institutional to community based care. Indeed, although overall rates of homicide have increased, those committed by people with serious mental distress form a steadily declining proportion of the total (Taylor and Gunn, 1999). In the UK, a recent survey showed that only 5% of those responsible for homicides had a diagnosis of schizophrenia (Shaw et al., 2006) and in New Zealand, the proportion of all homicides committed by the 'mentally abnormal' group fell from 19.5% in 1970 to 5% in 2000 (Simpson et al., 2004). Interestingly, the degree of moral panic around the risks posed by those with mental distress seems to be more prominent in Britain, America, Australia and New Zealand – but less so in continental Europe (Ramon, 2005).

In Britain, stoked both by selective and prejudicial media reporting and government positioning in relation to the public order agenda, the control of 'risk' came to be seen as the paramount duty of mental health professionals, displacing the duty to promote positive outcomes for people experiencing mental distress (Holloway, 1996). Seeking to minimise risk, rather than assessing need or promoting recovery, formed the underpinning rationale for the introduction of the Care Programme Approach (Department of Health, 1990). Within social care services, as budgets have tightened, there has been a switch from 'need' to 'risk' as the effective criterion of eligibility (Kemshall, 2002) – again privileging an obsession with possible harm over any commitment to providing therapeutic benefit.

The dominant discourse around risk tends to pathologise the individual where irrationality becomes conflated with the idea of inherent 'dangerousness'. Risks are seen as only lying within the person, rather than also in their wider social and environmental context; and the solution is seen as controlling the person (by whatever means), rather than examining what may be external sources of danger, exploitation or stress. We can easily lose sight of the fact that people with mental distress are more likely to be victims of violence than perpetrators (Social Exclusion Unit, 2004).

In a more general sense, a risk discourse that sets people up as different, incomprehensible and potentially dangerous inevitably leads to a practice that is, at best, paternalistic and, at worst, punitive and unnecessarily coercive. If practitioners work from the implicit assumption that people with mental distress constitute a danger to the general public, they are likely to reinforce rather than challenge barriers of stigma. Ongoing rituals of risk assessment may impact adversely on people's already vulnerable sense of self – leading them to internalise messages of their own inherent badness and harmfulness to others. The consequent impact in terms of social exclusion and damage to people's self-esteem may have the unintended consequence of exacerbating their mental distress and undermining their capability to manage potentially risky situations.

Prediction of risk and its limitations

There is no evidence to suggest that the current obsession with risk, and the increasing diversion of energy into practices of risk assessment and risk management, have actually resulted in any overall increase in safety for people with mental distress, their families or the wider public. In particular instances, risk-oriented practice may be helpful, perhaps in prompting a worker to ask about suicidal feelings in a situation where otherwise this would have not been discussed. However, in other instances, it may lead to a practice which is defensive, agency- not user-centred, and profoundly alienating to those experiencing acute mental distress. Such alienation may actually increase risks to both those experiencing mental distress and the wider public. Many people quickly learn not to talk to professionals about the voice in their head that is telling them to act violently for fear of what the service response is likely to be – and instead do their best to manage things on their own.

The whole risk-minimisation agenda has been driven by a fruitless quest to predict and prevent 'low-incidence/high-impact' risks such as homicide. Unfortunately, actuarial approaches to predicting risk are of little use in practice as there is little correlation between any form of psychiatric diagnosis and the likelihood of committing assault (Hiday, 2006; Monahan, 1993). Instead, this correlates more strongly with previous use of violence and, to a lesser extent, with a range of social and demographic factors that are not directly related to mental distress (such as age, gender, area of residence, educational attainment, poor social integration or alcohol and drug misuse). This makes it somewhat inappropriate to give mental health practitioners responsibility for assessing the risk of potential criminal behaviour towards others. The only exception to this is the very specific experience of 'command hallucinations' – internal voices that may urge one to commit acts of violence against self or others. Even here, prediction is of little value as most people will choose not to act on these commands – and empowerment relative to one's voices, rather than external regulation and surveillance, may provide the most effective strategy for managing such experiences (Birchwood et al., 2000).

Research has shown that even where, using all the available evidence, a particular sub-group of mental health service users had been identified as 'high risk', the great majority of these (over 80%) did not actually go on to commit an act of violence – and one-third of reported incidents of violence committed by the wider cohort were found to have involved those service users who had been deemed to be at low risk (Shergill and Szmukler, 1998). As Petch argues, 'The stark reality is that however good our tools for risk assessment become, ... professionals will not be able to make a significant impact on public safety' (2001, p. 203).

Overall, time invested in filling out risk-prediction scores must be seen as time taken away from engaging with the real issues faced by service users – some of which, if overlooked, may actually build up to the point where they may trigger violence or self-harm (Barker and Buchanan-Barker, 2004). A consistent picture that emerges from homicide enquiries is not that risk pro-formas were not completed, but that service users or carers were not listened to, were inappropriately refused services or discharged from services, or that practitioners failed to communicate effectively with one another or with other members of people's support systems. An overall analysis indicates that more deaths could be prevented by improving mental health provision across the board, rather than by seeking to target interventions on the basis of risk assessments (Munro and Rumgay, 2000).

From 'risk minimisation' to 'risk taking'

In the 1990s, the dominant approach to risk in mental health was that it was part of a professional duty of care to *minimise* the risk that certain individuals posed to themselves or others – as argued in the official report on the homicide of Jonathan Zito (Blom Cooper et al., 1995). However, this approach has been criticised (see, for example, Crowe and Carlyle, 2003). First, it sets up practitioners as somehow being 'in charge' of people with mental distress who are living in the community – which raises quite unrealistic expectations as to what power or influence practitioners may have over people and their situations. Secondly, it undermines collaboration and encourages a 'cotton-wool' approach in which people are likely to be overmedicated and discouraged from taking any steps towards reclaiming control over their lives and moving towards recovery.

In contrast to this, there is an emerging paradigm of positive risk-taking, as put forward in the Ten Essential Shared Capabilities (Department of Health, 2004). This offers a new orientation for professional practice that is much more in line with recovery principles. It relocates discussions of risk within the discourse of ordinary-life risk taking – no longer defining people as inherently 'other' and, because of this, inherently dangerous. Instead of risk always being seen negatively, a more balanced approach invites practitioners to see risks as often linked to opportunities and the potential to grow and change. Journeys of recovery are hardly ever risk free: indeed, taking personal risks may be seen as an essential component of any process of exploration and discovery (Stickley and Felton, 2006).

Within this paradigm, practitioners are no longer set up in opposition to service users, policing their behaviour and potentially reacting defensively to any attempt by them to break free from their containment within the mental health system. An alternative approach is offered in which the practitioner can take the role of ally, helping to explore with people what they want out of life and make an informed evaluation of any potential risks that may be associated with this (Felton and Stacey, 2008). Instead of seeking to minimise risk as an end in itself, there is a focus on what is an 'acceptable' level of risk, both for the person and for those around them. This assessment is not something that tries to be objective or scientific but involves a subjective engagement with what matters to people. Some goals may be so important to a person, in terms of their aspirations or building their sense of self-esteem, that they may wish to contemplate potentially serious risks such as a relapse into acute mental distress or a temporary escalation of self-harming behaviours.

While practitioners may sometimes need to be a little challenging – for example, if a person is discounting a possible area of risk that experience suggests could recur – they must also, in many instances, be willing to stand back and allow people to make their own choices and risk making their own mistakes: 'We must have the opportunity to try and to fail and to try again ... In order to support the recovery process, mental health professionals must not rob us of our opportunity to fail' (Deegan, 1996, p. 97).

Interestingly, when people experiencing mental distress have been interviewed about their experiences of risk assessment, a commonly voiced concern has been that, although they recognised risks and wanted help to reduce risk, it was practitioners who seemed awkward or frightened of entering into a full and open discussion of such issues (Langan and Lindow, 2004).

Safeguarding: what actually makes a situation safer?

While risk taking provides a framework for evaluating situations in which people may intentionally be taking personal risks, a broader approach to safeguarding also needs to take account of any risks of harm that may arise from factors that are more outside people's awareness or control – including the 'riskiness' of their social environment and the perhaps unanticipated consequences of professional interventions. Forms of potential harm may include:

- self-neglect;
- self-harm or suicide;
- violence towards others;
- being a victim of violence or harassment;
- breakdown of social or family relationships, or social isolation;
- exploitation or abuse by others;
- damage to physical health due to lifestyle (or side effects of medication);
- adverse mental health consequences resulting from professional interventions (such as compulsory detention).

Once we have a picture of what types of potential harm may be relevant, we may start to make sense of the underlying dynamics: what may be factors which either increase the level of risk or promote safety (see Table 10.1). Unsurprisingly, many of the factors that may increase risk of harm are the same sorts of factors that contribute to stress and vulnerability; and the factors that increase safety tend to correspond with those which enable recovery.

Table 10.1 Factors that may influence level of risk

	Factors that may increase risk of harm	Factors that may increase safety
Social variables	External stress factors or 'triggers', e.g. ● relationship difficulties ● being subject to stigma and discrimination ● social isolation ● poverty, poor housing ● feeling trapped, rejected or humiliated ● noisy or high-stimulation environments ● excessive demands or expectations ● insensitive or alienating professional interventions	Supportive environment, e.g. ● trusting and supportive relationships – preferably not just depending on one key person ● ability to control levels of stimulation and external demands ● safe and comfortable spaces to be ● options and choices
Personal variables	● particular sensitivities or internal 'trigger points' (related to personal vulnerabilities) ● feeling disconnected from or misperceiving external reality ● voices, beliefs or other experiences that lead to potentially harmful urges or impulses ● feelings of helplessness and hopelessness	● personal efficacy ● self-esteem and trust towards others ● self-awareness and understanding ● self-management strategies

Safeguarding is not about some (essentially futile) attempt at prediction, but is about gaining a dynamic understanding of the current situation – as far as possible in collaboration with all those involved. It is generally not one factor on its own that is significant; it is the interaction of personal and social variables within a situation that can escalate, or de-escalate the level of risk. For example, people may find that their particular distress experiences impair their cognitive or emotional abilities to 'read' social situations correctly – and hence their ability to keep themselves (or others) safe. Alongside this, certain social situations may trigger feelings, voices or impulses that, if acted upon, could lead to harmful outcomes. Such tendencies may be compounded by more general environmental factors, such as poor housing conditions, difficult neighbours or social stigmatisation. Such an interactive understanding may highlight problematic circumstances and issues that, if addressed, may prevent stresses getting to the point where people may become at risk of significant harm.

Safeguarding in practice

In the longer term, safety is best assured through people regaining control over their own lives, building their resilience and having good networks of support around them. From this position, they are best able to manage both external threats or triggers and potentially difficult impulses from within – and to call upon the help of others as necessary.

However, in the short term, safeguarding may involve the effective mobilisation of systems of *protective* power around a person with mental distress, together with interventions or strategies that address those factors that may be 'winding up' or threatening the situation. Protective power is likely to work best when the person is actively involved in identifying and dealing with potential risks. This requires an ethos of good and clear communication (including sharing anxieties and conflicting views) and providing support to all those involved.

What may make the greatest difference in practice is maintaining trusting and confiding relationships – in particular keeping open 'bridges' with the person experiencing mental distress (Barker and Buchanan-Barker, 2004). A person may be dealing with very challenging inner experiences – perhaps a feeling that they would be better off dead, or a voice that is telling them that a family member is possessed by the Devil – but the level of risk involved will depend greatly on their relationships with key others. If they feel able to confide in practitioners, family or friends, and discuss strategies for managing such experiences, the likelihood of any harm occurring will be much less than if the person is isolated. Safety nets based on close and supportive relationships can provide a much better alternative to the use of compulsion in 'holding' many potentially risky situations.

However, working towards this, particularly in a situation of crisis or conflict, may be far from straightforward. The process may need to start with separate conversations between the practitioner and each of those who are involved, and then bringing the various perspectives together by negotiating (where possible) for these to be shared with the other parties. Such processes can be much easier where it has been possible to do some advance planning – learning from previous experiences of crisis in order to devise an agreed way of trying to handle future crises – for example, by putting together an Advanced Directive (see Chapter 11).

Where advance planning has not been possible, a retrospective exploration of previous situations may be helpful in identifying what factors may influence the *trajectory* of risk – what may increase the potential for harm or help to bring the situation back under control. Making sense of the dynamics of risk in this way is of much more practical value than a static 'tick-box' actuarial analysis: it is this that will tell us whether further steps may be needed to safeguard the situation.

Coercion and compulsory detention

Most advanced countries have legislative frameworks which permit the use of compulsion as a last resort in managing situations of unacceptable risk – although there can be an unhelpful blurring of issues of safety and treatment. Within English mental health law, there is no provision for simply holding someone in a place of safety while their needs are assessed. All forms of detention also allow the administration of compulsory medical treatment which, given the research evidence in relation to early intervention and crisis resolution, may result in unnecessary and even counter-productive use of medication (see Chapter 8).

International comparisons across Europe suggest at least a five-fold variation in the use of compulsion (Hoyer, 2008; Zinkler and Priebe, 2002) and, in England, Black patients are nearly four times as likely as White patients to be compulsorily detained (Singh et al., 2007). Such huge variations cannot easily be explained by differences in people's inherent dangerousness: instead, it must largely reflect variations in public attitudes, service orientations and professional practice, including ingrained racism within services (Browne, 1997). Whereas the dominant human rights discourse of the early 1980s enshrined the principle of the 'least restrictive alternative' in the 1983 Mental Health Act in England and Wales, this has been silenced by the subsequent moral panics about mental health and risk in the 1990s. It has become an area where, perhaps somewhat surprisingly, European human rights law has become subservient to medical opinion and high rates of incarceration have not been contested (Richardson, 2008).

The potentially excessive use of compulsion represents the endpoint of a broader spectrum of coercive practice in which people are implicitly or explicitly threatened that unless they accede to the professionals' perspective on risk management (usually medication compliance), compulsory powers may be invoked (Szmukler and Appelbaum, 2008). As a consequence, many people experiencing more serious forms of mental distress, far from being encouraged to become collaborative partners in discussions around positive risk-taking and safeguarding, are disempowered by a coercive mental health practice – one which increasingly stigmatises them as being both inherently dangerous and inherently irresponsible.

A particularly controversial area has been the development of compulsory treatment in the community, which has been seen by many as a basic infringement of human rights. Research would suggest that those who may sometimes lack capacity to make judgements and may perhaps be a little chaotic – but who are not fundamentally averse to engaging with mental health services (and actually pose relatively low safety issues) – are those who may report satisfaction with 'low-level' compulsory arrangements (Swartz et al., 2004). Such arrangements can also be appreciated by families (Mullen et al., 2006) – although the main advantage may be through their indirect impact on service providers in ensuring that people actually receive the community services that they need. However, there is little overall evidence to suggest any systematic benefits arising from compulsory treatment in the community – for example, in terms of reducing hospital admissions (Kiseley et al., 2004). In many instances, those who comply with such orders probably do not need them in the first place, and those who are more seriously non-compliant will tend not to change their behaviour unless faced with the sanction of compulsory hospital admission.

If compulsion is just to be used as strategy of last resort, every effort should be made to find alternatives that may be acceptable and negotiable with the person. This requires the existence of alternative environments, such as crisis houses, so that treatment in an inpatient hospital setting is not the only available option. Where there has been prior involvement with services, people may draw up their own Advance Directives, in conjunction with professional helpers, stating how they would wish to be supported in the event of future crises. These have been shown to be effective in reducing compulsory admissions (Swanson et al., 2008), probably through engendering a better understanding within the professional team as to people's preferences and what might work as alternative approaches to safeholding within a crisis situation.

Experiences of coercion: safeholding or oppression?

Loss of capacity is never total – even if one is too unsafe to look after oneself, one may nevertheless have knowledge and preferences in terms of treatment options that should be respected wherever possible. It is therefore important to minimise the degree to which control is taken away from people. However, in practice, professional teams often assume that, once someone is compulsorily detained, they do not need to be treated with the same courtesies as informal patients, or consulted about courses of treatment or plans of care. This loss of respect, coupled with potentially invasive forms of intervention, may greatly increase the traumatic consequences of mental distress (see Chapter 7).

Relatively little research has been done on the impact of coercion on those who have been subjected to it – and whether, in the longer run, its use enhances or diminishes levels of safety. Any understanding of the experience must start with an analysis of power relations: does the imposition of control feel like the application of *protective* power, or does it come over as predominantly *oppressive*, intrusive or demeaning? Small-scale research into people's experience of compulsion indicates that, for a minority, it may feel like safeholding at a time when they were seriously out of control and at risk. Although they may have resisted it at the time, with hindsight they may be clear that it had been right to intervene (Barnes et al., 2000). What can make a difference may include:

- being offered respect and dignity as a person;
- being given an explanation of what is happening and opportunities for dialogue (and expression of feelings), both before and after a detention order is signed;
- being given some limited degree of choice wherever this may be possible;
- a positive experience of the forms of treatment and care that are offered;
- independent advocacy.

However, for the majority, the impact may be rather more adverse and long-lasting than many practitioners may realise. Detention and compulsory treatment could be experienced as so invasive and abusive that it further undermined an already fragile sense of self or self-esteem. It could construct an aura of dangerousness around the person that resulted in family or friends backing away, thereby doing long-term damage to their networks of social support. It could also damage trust and willingness to co-operate with professionals – again on a long-term basis – with people choosing to keep profes-

sionals at a distance and no longer confiding in them any information that might lead to the possibility of further compulsory
detention.

Thus, although coercion and compulsory detention may offer a
short-term solution to managing risk, it may have an impact on the
person's mental health, their social isolation and their engagement
with mental health services which may render them (and the wider
public) at greater risk in the longer term. This strengthens the
argument that a systematic approach needs to be taken to reduce the
use of compulsion and coercive approaches to risk management by:

- maintaining collaborative relationships that provide a 'bridge' to
  people who are potentially at risk;
- providing accessible and user-friendly crisis services so that people do not 'fall through the net';
- planning ahead for potential future crises and using Advance
  Directives where appropriate;
- independent advocacy to review whether professionals may have
  imposed a more restrictive or coercive alternative than was necessary under the circumstances.

Summary of key points

- A mental health diagnosis is not a significant predictor of
  violence and the proportion of homicides committed by
  those diagnosed with mental illness is falling.
- Actuarial approaches to predicting risk have no practical
  value in mental health.
- Risk taking provides a useful approach to working with
  intentional risk.
- Safeguarding requires an analysis of the interaction of
  personal and situational factors that may be increasing or
  reducing levels of risk.
- Variation in rates of compulsory detention suggest that
  many instances of coercion could be avoided – particularly
  for Black people.
- A more collaborative approach, using Advanced Directives
  and alternatives to hospital, can reduce the need for
  compulsory admissions.
- Even if they are compulsorily detained, people should be
  treated with respect and offered choice wherever possible.

Further reading

Felton, A., & Stacey, G. (2008). *Positive risk taking: A framework for practice*. In T. Stickley & T. Bassett (eds), *Learning About Mental Health Practice*. Chichester: Wiley.

Kemshall, H. (2002). *Risk, Social Policy and Welfare*. Buckingham: Open University Press.

Langan, J., & Lindow, V. (2004). *Living With Risk: Mental Health Service User Involvement in Risk Assessment and Management*. Bristol: Policy Press.

11 | Assessment, Action Planning and self-directed support

Assessment is a crucial element of professional practice, and experience demonstrates that time and thought invested in doing this well is more than repaid in outcomes achieved. A failure to understand the history and dynamics of a situation, or to locate it in a wider social context, can result in a great deal of resources being put in, potentially over a long period of time, to little avail in terms of achieving recovery or a better quality of life. Indeed services, however well-intentioned, may actually act as a 'buffer' between problems and solutions, ignoring strengths and potential, propping up arrangements that may be far from satisfactory, encouraging dependence on services and inducting people into long-term 'careers' as mental health service users.

In this chapter, I will discuss inclusive processes of assessment and link these to approaches to Action Planning that come from Person Centred Planning and from the recovery movement. These may then form the basis of imaginative and flexible arrangements for self-directed support.

Process of assessment

Fundamental to a good assessment are principles of partnership and inclusiveness which can capitalise on the expertise and understanding of those directly involved (including family, friends and other allies). The primary role of the practitioner is to facilitate and not to dominate – to enable people to tell their stories and make connections, rather than structuring the interaction on the basis of a set of predetermined questions that impose a particular way of seeing upon everyone involved. This approach corresponds with the Exchange Model of social care assessment (Smale et al., 1998).

However, one of the most formidable barriers to good practice in assessment can be frameworks of performance management which impose a target of having a document (however superficial) in place within a specified time period. This reduces assessment to a one-sided process of information gathering and leaves insufficient time to grasp what is really going on. This may lead into a formulaic response based on a standard menu of options which may turn out to be irrelevant to people's possibility of recovery. If a situation were straightforward enough to be assessed in two or three meetings, then it is unlikely to be one that would require any complex professional intervention.

Unfortunately, such assessments can set the tone of subsequent working relationships between service user and practitioner. An imperative to complete agency documentation does not allow for the sort of exploration and relationship building that is at the core of successful partnership working. It maintains the idea of assessment as something that is done *on* people rather than done *with* people – a practice that is more likely to be experienced as oppressive than enabling. It situates the professional as 'expert' and renders the service user (and those around them) powerless to make sense of and resolve their particular difficulties – and may thereby actively impede the process of recovery.

A comprehensive assessment may take months – as people may only start to feel comfortable sharing more serious issues as they build trust in the practitioner and develop a more confiding relationship. The processes of change, discovery and learning that characterise a recovery journey may lead to the gradual unfolding of a clearer understanding of what people may need and where they are going. Conversely, an assessment process that enables an inclusive dialogue may also bring about change in how people see themselves and relate to each other. Getting difficult issues out into the open may be all that is needed – people may then be able to resolve them in their own ways with little further need for professional help. Thus, while there can tend to be a separation within professional protocols between assessment and intervention, this distinction can be somewhat arbitrary in practice.

The fundamental principles for good practice in the process of assessment are:

- Involve everyone who is connected to the situation, both to build an understanding of what is going on and to maximise resources for finding solutions.
- Develop ways of understanding the situation through dialogue and exchange of ideas.
- Do not assume that there is only one way of understanding the situation, or that any one way of understanding is inherently better than any other. Sharing insights based on lived experience

and theory can provide a fertile basis for developing a range of ways of seeing – and differences can be creative.

● Be prepared to reassess as situations – and working relationships – develop and change.

Initial assessment: eligibility, need and risk

In many practice settings, a key task of assessment is to establish whether or not a person should receive a service or be allocated a budget by which they may organise their own supports. Within social care, eligibility is usually based on criteria of need (what levels of support and resource may people require in order to live as independently as possible) or on the degree of risk that they may pose to self or others. Within health care, eligibility is usually based on being given a medical diagnosis which then opens up certain specified options in terms of treatment and care. Within mental health, which uncomfortably straddles both health and social care, there can either be two essentially separate modalities of assessment operating in parallel, or an uneasy amalgam of the two.

As they stand, neither approach quite fits mental health. As we have seen in Chapter 2, mental 'illness' diagnoses are poor indicators of social functioning – and hence do not work well as measures of need or risk. The social care model implicitly assumes that needs and risks relate to a level of impairment – where the impairment itself is seen as a given. Again, this model does not work easily within the context of mental health, where a person's distress is not a given but relates to their life experiences and social circumstances – and where, if these issues are responded to, recovery may be possible.

Nevertheless, we do need to distinguish whether or not a person is experiencing a significant level of mental distress and hence whether they may need (specialist) services in order to avert more serious distress or support their recovery. There is a need to differentiate between the everyday misery, frustration and unease that we may feel as we grapple with life's difficulties and the different order of experiences that may emerge if our coping mechanisms start to break down – or themselves become problematic. A screening tool, such as that shown in Table 8.2 (Chapter 8), may be particularly helpful here.

The notion of *complaint* provides a much more practical alternative to medical diagnosis (see Chapter 2). It is couched in everyday language and concepts; it describes directly the form of experience that a person may be finding difficult and the impact that it may be having on their life (and on those around them); and formulates this in a way that empowers the person and those around them to

Table 11.1 Questions to answer in an initial social assessment

1	How is mental distress being manifested (e.g. hearing voices, self-harming or becoming locked into feelings of depression or anxiety)?
2	Why is this a problem and how is it affecting everyday living for the person and those around them (e.g. hearing voices may only be a problem if the voices are nasty or excessively powerful)?
3	What stresses or life events may be contributing to current difficulties?
4	To what degree does the person feel able to control or manage their distress experiences? What are their best available coping strategies?
5	Is anyone at risk of harm and, if so, what may help to ensure greater safety?
6	What would those within the situation see as a positive outcome or a solution to their current difficulties?

become involved in looking for solutions. Describing a complaint does not involve shoehorning a person's experience into some arbitrary system of classification. Instead, it may be best expressed as a brief narrative which includes responses to the questions outlined in Table 11.1.

Such a formulation of the complaint in terms of *distress-in-context* provides an initial framework by which to consider eligibility for mental health services – and for determining the priority of response that may be needed in terms of agency criteria of need and risk. However, without a more thorough (and potentially ongoing) process of assessment, this may not provide much of a guide as to what forms of help may be beneficial in promoting recovery.

A comprehensive mental health assessment

While an initial assessment necessarily needs to focus on 'what is wrong', a more comprehensive assessment needs to counterbalance this with an emphasis on strengths, aspirations and resources. It also needs to explore the meanings that people attach to their experiences and the relationships between mental distress, life events and social circumstances – both past and present (see Table 11.2). In line with Department of Health guidance on the Care Programme Approach, it is important to view 'a person "in the round", seeing and supporting them in their individual diverse roles and the needs they have, including: family; parenting; relationships; housing; employment; leisure; education; creativity; spirituality; self-management and self-nurture' (Department of Health, 2008, p. 7).

Table 11.2 Areas to cover in a comprehensive social assessment

1	The presenting complaint and what this *means* to everyone involved.
2	What may have led up, or contributed, to the current situation – life events, social circumstances and particular stresses (e.g. what was going on in your life when you first started to hear voices?).
3	The current social context – culture, occupation, housing, income, access to social capital; experiences of discrimination or social exclusion.
4	Family and interpersonal relationships: ● what relationships are supportive and affirmative? ● where may there be tensions or conflicts? ● what connections may have been lost?
5	The impact of experiences on sense of self and social identities.
6	Strengths, resources and coping strategies.
7	Power relations, personal efficacy and opportunities for mobilising *co-operative* and *protective* power.
8	The way forward: ideas and aspirations of all those involved in the situation.

Addressing each of these areas can open up a dialogue which puts together people's experience (and their ways of seeing it) with the reflections and theoretically based ideas that the practitioner may bring. As can be seen, questions 2 to 7 link closely with particular theoretical models and perspectives that have been developed throughout this book.

As with the initial assessment, a comprehensive social assessment can best be constructed as a shared narrative (with room for differences of perspective within it). Practical tools such as ecomaps (Hartman, 1995) can be particularly helpful in exploring the context of social relationships and access to social capital – and it can be empowering if those involved draw these up for themselves so that they can reflect on their social worlds as they see them. Although much in the current situation may seem bleak and distressing, it is important to hold, within the discussion, a prospect of a future that allows room for aspirations.

Exploring what may have led up to a current mental health difficulty may help to identify issues that may still need to be resolved in some way – or, at least, acknowledged. By gaining a clearer picture of current relationships, social connections and power relations, we may see not only what people may currently have (or have access to), but also the resources, supports and opportunities what they may have lost or may never have had. This can help to set the agenda for socially focused action planning – looking at how best to maximise people's control over their situation, their opportunities to access or hold on to valued social roles and their ability to negotiate effective strategies for support and safety.

Family Group Conferences

Family Group Conferencing provides an inclusive and potentially empowering approach to planning and decision making, and has been developed out of cultural practices within the Maori communities in New Zealand (Marsh and Crow, 1998). It has initially been used in relation to decision making around children, but is starting to be applied within the context of mental health (Wright, 2008). It entails bringing together all those who are (or could be) involved in a person's welfare – not necessarily just immediate and extended family, but also friends, neighbours or other allies – to talk through aspirations and concerns. A facilitator, who brings no preconceived ideas as to possible ways forward, enables the participants to come up with an agreed plan as to how to provide support, ensure safety and work towards desired outcomes. The principal advantage of this approach is that it can secure the active engagement of the whole social system in providing support and ensuring safety – mobilising *co-operative* and *protective* power in a way that cannot be delivered so effectively by a more individualised approach.

Whether this is the most appropriate way of undertaking assessment and Action Planning depends on whether the person with mental distress is at a point where they would feel able to participate – which, in turn, depends both on their mental state (in terms of ability to concentrate and formulate their views) and on their perception of how supportive family or other relationships may be. At its best, this may provide a forum in which they can be heard and understood in a way that they have not been before. At its worst, it may set up a situation that is intimidating and antagonistic – or where the person will simply be patronised and put down by other family members – which will simply reinforce their powerlessness.

It is therefore an approach which needs to be used sensitively at points where key decisions may need to be made. It is likely to work best when someone is not too 'unwell' and should always be considered as a potential format for undertaking Action Planning.

Action Planning

A comprehensive social assessment provides the basis for organising actions and supports that will enable people to deal more effectively with crisis situations and take charge of their recovery. Unlike a Care Plan, an Action Plan does not imply that people will need to be 'cared for' or have decisions made about them by more competent others. Nor does it assume that any impairment is long term, but sets out a process geared towards recovery and a possible 'exit strategy' from services at some point in the future.

Action Planning has emerged out of the recovery movement. It places the person with mental distress at the heart of decision making so that they can retain as much control over their life as they are able. Whereas Care Planning tends to focus on what people cannot do for themselves, Action Planning foregrounds people's strengths and aspirations as well as identifying areas where they may need support. Its philosophy shares much in common with Person Centred Planning and emphasises:

- empowerment;
- choices, abilities and aspirations;
- learning through shared action and reflecting on experience;
- problem solving and finding creative solutions or coping strategies (and not assuming that people need 'care' services);
- involving family and friends;
- working on personal and relationship issues;
- negotiating personal and social support;
- developing social capital – involving work with groups, networks and communities as well as with individuals;
- taking on (or reclaiming) valued social roles;
- achieving a balance between positive risk taking and ensuring safety.

There are a range of practical frameworks and tools for implementing an Action Planning approach. Specific to mental health, there is *Wellness Recovery Action Planning* (WRAP), which provides a comprehensive and detailed framework for a person to reflect on and take charge of their mental health, including actions to maintain wellbeing and ways of dealing with setbacks or crises should these occur (Copeland, 1997). Although originating in the USA, this is being adapted and used extensively in the UK. Other frameworks and tools from Person Centred Planning provide ways of focusing on goals and aspirations (Sanderson, 2000). Such approaches can feed directly into statutory frameworks such as the Care Programme Approach – but enable the service user to be in charge of their plan and what goes into it.

Any approach to Action Planning in mental health needs to take account of the variability of people's experience over time – people may need specific Action Plans in relation to *prevention* and *early warning,* dealing with *crises,* enabling *recovery* and maintaining *wellness.*

Early Warning and Relapse Prevention Plans

Both at the stage of Early Intervention, and when anticipating the possibility of relapses or setbacks further down the line, it may be important to develop an Action Plan which focuses on identifying and managing particular sources of stress and responding to the first warning signs that one's coping mechanisms may be starting to break down. Such a Plan may usefully involve, not just the person but also family and friends who may be in a position to spot first when things are starting to go wrong – once they know what to look out for.

The assessment may identify particular forms of stress to which the person may be sensitive, or life events (such as a relationship break-up) which may be hard for them to deal with. Where someone has already experienced previous episodes of distress, it may be helpful for them to reflect in detail on what may have led up to these – ideally in collaboration with those who are close to them. Out of this may emerge valuable insights as to what may be particular signs that they are not coping well – signs that may be unique to them and which, taken on face value, might not be seen by others as matters of great concern. For example, their characteristic 'relapse signature' may involve getting up late, going to church more often, or perhaps appearing a little rude or abrupt.

Where someone is identified as being potentially at risk, an Action Plan can be developed which may focus on:

- Maintaining social connections and activities where possible – including involvement in work, education and social and family networks. This may include providing support to wider social systems.
- Being alert to when the stress of particular social situations may cross a 'trigger' threshold and start to threaten their mental health.
- Identifying trusted friends or family members who could watch out for warning signs.

- Having ways of talking about concerns and enlisting back-up without starting a panic.
- Implementing agreed 'what to do if ...' strategies for managing or avoiding current sources of stress – perhaps negotiating reduced involvement or temporary time out from particular responsibilities.

Crisis Plans

When someone is experiencing an initial mental health crisis, there may be little possibility of advanced planning – so a plan may have to be developed 'on the hoof' on the basis of an understanding of the situation that is continually unfolding. Key components of such a Crisis Plan may include:

1. Actions to *hold* the situation in terms of establishing boundaries and support systems that provide structure and safety. This may involve a crisis resolution team and/or family or friends providing home-based support, or the person moving temporarily to a crisis house or hospital.
2. Liaising with employers, social networks, extended family and others to inform them of the current situation, negotiating temporary time out of current responsibilities, and agreeing ongoing means of keeping contact so that involvements can be resumed as soon as the person is able.
3. Identifying and working with any personal, social and relationship issues that may have emerged as part of the crisis – utilising the 'window of opportunity' for acknowledgement and resolution that is presented by the crisis (see Chapter 8).

Where someone has had the opportunity to reflect on previous experiences of mental health crisis, they may be able to be more prescriptive as to what would work best for them. WRAP provides an excellent framework for formulating an Advance Crisis Plan – ideally through discussion and negotiation with family, friends and professionals. This may take the form of an informal agreement, although some may wish to draw up an Advance Directive – which, in turn, could be linked to a budget for self-directed support. As we saw in Chapter 10, such a proactive approach can reduce the likelihood of compulsory detention or treatment (Swanson et al., 2008).

Recovery Plans

Typically, a Recovery Plan would follow on from a Crisis Plan. It starts to envision life beyond mental distress and is likely to involve a twin-track approach of developing social engagement alongside support for a more personal journey of discovery, adjustment and reclaiming control over one's life

There are a number of planning tools which may be helpful, such as *Personal Futures Planning* or *Planning Alternative Tomorrows and Hope* (PATH) (Sanderson, 2000). The Mental Health Recovery Star (MacKeith and Burns, 2010) invites people to identify their personal goals and progress in relation to ten 'life domains' (Figure 11.1).

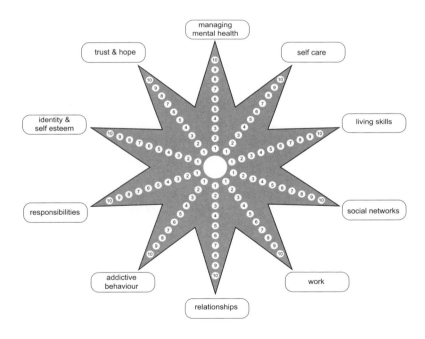

Figure 11.1 The Mental Health Recovery Star

Source: MacKeith and Burns, 2010. Reproduced with permission.

Some people find it helpful to map out longer-term goals and aspirations and then work out a series of incremental steps that lead towards this – along similar lines to a Task Centred Approach (Doel and Marsh, 2003). This may need to be over an extended timescale if people have experienced more serious episodes of mental distress. Within such an approach, a useful guideline is that at least half of the work towards the achievement of a given step should be made by the person her/himself. Initial steps may need to be deliberately unambitious – as succeeding in a small endeavour starts a process of positive reinforcement, whereas failing at a greater task may undermine self-confidence and motivation. Built into such a plan needs to be an acknowledgement that progress is rarely smooth or linear – and that setbacks or changes of direction are not to be seen as 'failures' but as opportunities for learning and development.

Other people find such approaches too programmatic and pre-scriptive:

'I identify with the Nike slogan: "Just do it!" … *When I read about recovery written as goal-driven* … *that can only be written by practitioners because how many of us get up in the morning and say: How am I going towards my goals today? That is not something that you do.'* (Susanne, quoted in Borg and Davidson, 2008, p. 134)

By definition, recovery is a process that has to be owned by people themselves – so imposing any particular tool or planning approach is likely to be counterproductive. For some people, it is simply important to 'live in the now' – to feel and to experience – and it is out of this that will emerge their aspirations and sense of direction.

Keeping Well Plans

If and when the steep climb of someone's recovery journey is over, they may still need to take active steps to maintain their wellbeing and manage any ongoing experiences which could be problematic (such as mood swings or hearing voices). Using an approach such as WRAP can enable a very detailed reflection on what may make a difference in terms of staying well (Copeland, 1997). A Keeping Well Plan may include a focus on:

- achieving a healthy lifestyle (including a good diet, hobbies, regular exercise, and so on);
- having ways of keeping in touch with one's inner experience and dealing with feelings of unease as they arise;
- maintaining a network of allies or supporters to help deal with any problems of living;

- identifying and managing potential sources of social stress (including racism and other forms of social oppression);
- accessing wider networks of social capital;
- maintaining an active coping style, and deploying problem-solving and other capabilities that may contribute to resilience;
- being able to access informal and/or professional support quickly if one starts to dip.

For some people, maintaining wellbeing and social participation, and managing any ongoing distress experiences, may involve the continuation of certain low-level forms of support from mental health or other services. A small ongoing investment of time or resource may make a major difference in averting the possibility of relapse.

Self-directed support and personal budgets

A major innovation in service provision is the idea of self-directed support linked to personal budgets. Instead of the paternalism inherent in more traditional arrangements, in which practitioners assess people's needs and arrange the provision of services by which to meet them, people are increasingly being given opportunities to articulate their needs for themselves ('self-assessment') and determine how their financial entitlement should be spent. This is based on the principles of Independent Living (Deegan, 1992) and may be achieved through mechanisms such as Direct Payments, or more indirectly, with funds being placed with a care manager or an independent brokerage organisation – but with all decisions being made, as far as possible, by the service user (Brewis, 2007; Glasby and Littlechild, 2009).

In principle, this provides a very practical way of putting a person in charge of their own recovery by giving them effective control of a budget – which they may then use in potentially unconventional ways to fund actions and supports that they consider will be of most benefit to them. Where self-directed support has been piloted in the USA, it has tended to result in a shift of resources towards prevention and away from crisis response through people being able to set up easier access to services that help to maintain their wellbeing (Alakeson, 2007).

Due to the potential variability of people's mental states, many have been reluctant to make use of inflexible approaches such as Direct Payments where they would have to take full responsibility for managing finances and employing support workers. What many people prefer would be having the support of brokerage organisations that are able to vary the level of their input depending on people's mental capacity – from handing over full control when they are well, to managing monies in line with an agreed Advanced Directive when they are in crisis.

Experience from the USA suggests that if brokerage can be delivered by locally based peer-run organizations, it can be particularly effective (*ibid.*). This is because they:

- can link people together so as to enable peer support and to facilitate collective solutions to shared concerns or aspirations (perhaps by pooling individual budgets);
- can be embedded within particular communities and facilitate culturally sensitive forms of support;
- are trusted to advocate and manage things in a user-centred way when people are not feeling so well;
- provide employment opportunities where lived experience can be an asset.

As well as seeking flexibility in brokerage arrangements, people may need different allocations of resources depending on whether they are relatively well, in crisis, or in recovery. Specific budgets for self-directed support could be linked to the specific types of Action Plan that were outlined above, including:

- *Early Warning* or *Relapse Prevention Budgets* for those who are at risk of developing mental distress which would enable them to develop social capital, access social opportunities and manage identified areas of social stress – and bring in support quickly if they are starting to dip.
- *Crisis Budgets* which would kick in if someone has a crisis or a setback and fund the supports they have specified in an Advanced Directive. For many people, this is likely to involve community-based alternatives to acute inpatient care – which could reflect their cultural or other preferences.
- *Recovery Budgets* which would buy in supports or therapies to enable a person to achieve their goals in terms of recovery and social inclusion (see Coyle, 2009).
- *Keeping Well Budgets* which people could access in order to maintain their wellbeing. These may support them in maintaining aspects of social engagement or managing ongoing sources of social stress.

A focus on Action Planning and, where appropriate, self-directed support offers the possibility of 'light-touch' mental health services that enable rather than take over – which may not only be more effective in promoting recovery, but may also be more cost-effective in reducing the likelihood that people may become trapped in positions of long-term dependence within the mental health system.

Summary of key points

- Processes of assessment and Action Planning should be inclusive of family and friends, and involve dialogue and collaboration between practitioners and those with direct experience.
- Initial assessments establish eligibility and priority in terms of need and risk.
- Comprehensive assessments build a bigger picture of how distress may relate to social context, and what may be people's strengths and aspirations.
- People should be in charge of devising their own Action Plans, and may need specific plans to assist them in relation to:
    - prevention and early warning of relapse;
    - managing crises;
    - enabling recovery;
    - keeping well.
- Self-directed support provides a mechanism for people to take direct control of implementing their Action Plans.

Further reading

Assessment:
Smale, G., Tuson, G., Biehal, N., & Marsh, P. (1998) *Empowerment, Assessment, Care Management and the Skilled Worker* (2nd ed.). London: National Institute for Social Work.

Action planning:
Copeland, M.E. (1997) *Wellness Recovery Action Plan*. Brattleboro, VT: Peach Press.

Self-directed support:
Brewis, R. (2007) *A Voice and a Choice: Self-directed Support by People with Mental Health Problems*. Wythall: In-Control.
www.in-control.org.uk

12 | Concluding comments: putting social theory and research into practice

In this book, I have explored the compelling evidence of how social factors and experiences may contribute to mental distress – and how specific experiences of mental distress may be understood as a response to these. Addressing these issues (and how these may have been internalised) can be important if people are to be able to deal with and recover from mental health difficulties. Alongside this, I have also highlighted the importance of looking at the positive aspects of people's experiences, such as their personal resilience and their access to social capital and supportive interpersonal relationships. Nurturing and developing these may be crucial both in enabling people's recovery and in reducing the likelihood that experiences of unease will escalate into mental distress in the first place.

In order for research findings to be useful in guiding practice, we need a clearer theoretical understanding of the mechanisms whereby adverse social experiences may provoke journeys into mental distress, and more positive experiences can provide the foundations for recovery and wellbeing. Particularly in Chapters 5 and 7, I have outlined the basis for such an understanding – exploring how external and internal aspects of people's experience may link together, and developing conceptual models that bridge the rather separate perspectives of social and psychological theory. As we have seen, issues of power and powerlessness appear as a recurring underlying theme, shaping the construction of distress and the possibilities of recovery. However, further work needs to done to refine and develop such analytical frameworks, based on more extensive research and the distillation of the themes that emerge from people's stories.

As we understand more clearly the dynamics and interactions that lead people into and out of mental distress, it will also become clearer where social interventions and supports may most usefully be targeted in order to influence the pathways that people may follow.

Shifting the paradigm of practice

A social approach demands that we find ways of seeing and conceptualising the 'bigger picture' – understanding the dynamics of people's *situations* rather than just focusing on internal 'pathologies' (Nelson et al., 2001b). People's distress may be as much within their relationships and their social context as it is within their inner mental life – although these two aspects are likely to be intimately connected. Therefore, it is important to develop a 'whole systems' approach to practice that involves engaging at multiple system levels, including:

- *Micro level*: supporting people around their personal experience and inner struggles and conflicts; providing opportunities for choice and control; enabling people to develop their cognitive social capital.
- *Meso level*: working with family and friends to enhance interpersonal relationships; enabling people to access social capital and take on valued social roles.
- *Macro level*: promoting accepting communities and the infrastructure of social capital within them; engaging with social attitudes, media representations and wider policy discourses in order to challenge processes of stigmatisation and discrimination.

Whether one is involved in early intervention, crisis resolution or the longer-term support of recovery, it is important that practitioners embrace 'bigger picture' ways of understanding and responding to situations of mental distress. There is strong evidence to suggest that working with families, social networks and communities can be much more effective in promoting wellbeing and recovery than seeking just to resolve individual issues without changing the wider context in which they are situated.

Such a way of working runs counter to current tendencies within mental health services (and within social work) for a purely individualised focus that rarely moves beyond an engagement with immediate needs, risks and compliance with medical treatment. It involves making connections and working alliances outside the immediate confines of the mental health system – with mainstream services, employers, housing providers, communities and community leaders, policy makers, and so on.

However, the wider policy context may provide important levers for change – such as the Putting People First concordat and the New Horizons strategy for mental health within the English context (Department of Health, 2007, 2009), and potentially similar developments elsewhere. The emerging emphasis on wellbeing and social participation – and a recognition of the wider economic and social value of this – may also act as a driver towards the reorientation of services, and professional practice, in ways that give priority to the 'bigger picture' and an emphasis on building on strengths and resources both at an individual and at a community level.

Alongside this, another potential driver for change is the introduction of mechanisms for self-directed support such as personal budgets. These have the potential to shift the locus of control away from traditional vested professional interests and towards bottom-up change that reflects the aspirations of service users and carers – and to broaden people's horizons beyond the limitations of a life defined by mental health services. What may make a particular difference may be arrangements for brokerage and connection that enable the emergence (and funding) of collective as well as individualised opportunities for support and development.

Within this context, it is for practitioners, service users and carers to use the *evidence base* which demonstrates the importance of social factors, and a *value base* that is inspired by ideas of recovery and collaboration, in order to argue for the ongoing development of a social approach for working with people who may experience mental distress.

References

Addington, J., Addington, D., Jones, B., & Ko, T. (2001). Family intervention in an early psychosis program. *American Journal of Psychiatric Rehabilitation* 5: 272–86.

Ainsworth, M., Biehar, M., Waters, E., & Wall, S. (1978). *Patterns of attachment*. Hillsdale, NJ: Lawrence Erlbaum.

Alakeson, V. (2007). *The contribution of self-direction to improving the quality of mental health services*. US Department of Health and Human Services. http://aspe.hhs.gov/daltcp/reports/2007/Mhslfdir.htm

Aldridge, J., & Becker, S. (2003) *Children caring for parents with mental illness*. Bristol: Policy Press.

Alexander, A. (2008) *Understanding recovery*. In Realising Recovery Learning Materials. Scottish Recovery Network/NHS Education for Scotland. www.nes.scot.nhs.uk/mentalhealth/publications/documents/13875–NES-MentalHealth-Allmodules.pdf

American Psychiatric Association (1994). *Diagnostic, and statistical manual of mental disorders* (4th ed.) (DSM–IV). Washington, DC: APA.

Baker Miller, J. (1991). Women and power. In J. Jordan, A. Kaplan, J. Baker Miller, I. Stiver, & J. Surrey, *Women's growth in connection*. New York: Guilford.

Bandura, A. (1977). Self efficacy: Toward a unifying theory of behavioural change. *Psychological Review* 84: 191–315.

Barker P., & Buchanan-Barker, P. (2004). *Bridging – talking meaningfully about the care of people at risk*. http://www.tidal-model.co.uk/Bridging.htm

Barker, P., Campbell, P., & Davidson, B. (1999). *From the ashes of experience: Reflections on madness, survival, and growth*. London: Whurr.

Barnes, M., Davis, A., & Tew, J. (2000). Valuing experience: Users' experience of compulsion under the Mental Health Act 1983. *Mental Health Review* 5(3): 11–14.

Barnes, M., & Bowl, R. (2001). *Taking over the asylum: Empowerment, and mental health.* Basingstoke: Palgrave.

Bates, S., & Coren, E. (2006). *The extent, and impact of parental mental health problems on families, and the acceptability, accessibility, and effectiveness of interventions.* London: SCIE Systematic map report 1.

Bateson, G., Jackson, D., Haley, J., & Weakland, J. (1956). Toward a theory of schizophrenia. *Behavioral Science* 1: 251–64.

Beck, U. (1992). *The risk society.* London: Sage.

Becker, E. (1972). *The birth and death of meaning.* Harmondsworth: Penguin.

Becker, H. (1963). *Outsiders: Studies in the sociology of deviance.* New York: Free Press of Glencoe.

Bebbington, P. , Bhugra, D., Bhugra, T., Singleton, N., Farrell, M., Jenkins, R., Lewis, G., & Meltzer, H. (2004). Psychosis, victimisation, and childhood disadvantage: Evidence from the second British National Survey of Psychiatric Morbidity. *British Journal of Psychiatry* 185: 220–26.

Beck, A., Rush, A., Shaw, B., & Emery, G. (1979). *Cognitive therapy for depression.* New York: Guilford.

Bentall, R. (2003). *Madness explained: Psychosis, and human nature.* London: Penguin.

Bentall, R. (2004). Abandoning the concept of schizophrenia: The cognitive psychology of hallucinations & delusions. In J. Read, L. Mosher, & R. Bentall (eds), *Models of madness.* Hove: Brunner–Routledge.

Bentall, R., Corcoran, R., Howard, R., Blackwood, R., & Kinderman, P. (2001). Persecutory delusions. A review and theoretical integration. *Clinical Psychology Review* 21: 1143–92.

Beresford, P. (2003). *It's our lives: A short theory of knowledge, distanceand experience.* London: Citizen Press/Shaping Our Lives.

Bhugra, D, Leff, J., Mallett, R., & Mahy, G. (1999). First-contact incidence rate of schizophrenia in Barbados. *British Journal of Psychiatry* 175: 28–33.

Birchwood, M., Todd, P. , & Jackson, C. (1998). Early intervention in psychosis: the critical period hypothesis. *International Clinical Psychopharmacology* 13(suppl. 1): 31–40.

Birchwood, M., Meaden, A., Trower, P. , Gilbert, P. , & Plaistow, J. (2000). The power and omnipotence of voices: Subordination and entrapment by voices and significant others. *Psychological Medicine* 30: 337–44.

Blom Cooper L., Murphy, E., & Hally, H. (1995). *The falling shadow.* London: Duckworth.

Bola, J., Lehtinen, K., Cullberg, J., & Ciompi, L. (2009). Psychosocial treatment, antipsychotic postponement and low-dose medication strategies in first-episode psychosis: A review of the literature. *Psychosis* 1(1): 4–18.

Borg, M., & Davidson, L. (2008). The nature of recovery as lived in everyday experience. *Journal of Mental Health* 17(2): 129–40.

Borg, M., & Kristiansen, K. (2008). Working on the edge: The meaning of work for people recovering from severe mental distress in Norway. *Disability and Society* 23(5): 511–23.

Bourdieu, P. (1977). Cultural reproduction and social reproduction. In J. Karabel, & A.H. Halsey (eds), *Power and ideology in education*. New York: Oxford University Press, pp. 487–511.

Bourdieu, P. (1990). Structures, habitus, practices. In *The logic of practice*. Stanford, CA: Stanford University Press, pp. 52–79.

Bowlby, J. (1982). *Attachment and loss* (Vol. 1). London: Hogarth Press.

Boydell, J., van Os, J., McKenzie, K., Allardyce, J., Goel, R., McCreadie, R., & Murray, R. (2001) Incidence of schizophrenia in ethnic minorities in London: Ecological study into interactions with environment. *British Medical Journal* 323: 1–4.

Boyle, M. (2002). *Schizophrenia: A scientific delusion?* London: Routledge.

Bradshaw, W., Armour, M.P. , & Roseborough, D. (2007). Finding a place in the world: The experience of recovery from severe mental illness. *Qualitative Social Work* 6(1): 27–47.

Braye, S., & Preston-Shoot, M. (1995). *Empowering practice in social care*, Buckingham: Open University.

Brewis, R. (2007). A voice and a choice: Self-directed support by people with mental health problems. Wythall: In-Control. www.in-control.org.uk

Bridgett, C., & Polak, P. (2003). Social systems intervention and crisis resolution. Part 1: Assessment. *Advances in Psychiatric Treatment* 9: 424–31.

Brodsky, B.S., Cloitre, M., & Dulit, R.A. (1995). Relationship of dissociation to self-mutilation and childhood abuse in borderline personality disorder. *American Journal of Psychiatry* 152(12): 1788–92.

Brown G., & Harris, T. (1978). *The social origins of depression*. London: Tavistock.

Brown, G., Harris, T., & Hepworth, C. (1995). Loss, humiliation and entrapment among women developing depression: A patient and non-patient comparison. *Psychological Medicine* 25: 7–21.

Browne, D. (1997). *Black people and 'sectioning'*. London: Little Rock Publishing.

Browne, D. (2009). Black communities, mental health and the criminal justice system. In J. Reynolds, R. Muston, T. Heller, J. Leach, M. McCormick, J. Wallcraft, & M. Walsh (eds), *Mental health still matters*. Basingstoke: Palgrave Macmillan.

Burns, T., Catty, J. White, S., Becker, T., Koletis, M., Fioritti, A, Rossler, W., Tomov, T., Van Busschbach, J., Wiersma, D., & Lauber, C. (2009). The impact of supported employment and working on clinical and social functioning. *Schizophrenia Bulletin* 35(5): 949–58.

Campbell, P. (1996). Challenging loss of power. In J. Read, & J. Reynolds (eds), *Speaking our minds*. Basingstoke: Macmillan.

Caplan, G. (1965). *Principles of preventive psychiatry*. London: Tavistock.

Carling, P. (1995). *Return to community*. New York: Guilford.

Carr, S. (2005). 'The sickness label infected everything we said' – lesbian and gay perspectives on mental distress. In J. Tew (ed.), *Social perspectives in mental health*. London: Jessica Kingsley.

Castillo, H. (2000). You don't know what it is like. *Mental Health Care* 4(2): 42–3.

Chamberlin, J. (1997). A working definition of empowerment. *Psychiatric Rehabilitation Journal* 20(4): 43–6.

Clay, S., Schell, B., Corrigan, P. , & Ralph, R. (eds) (2005). *On our own, together: Peer programs for people with mental illness*. Nashville TN: Vanderbilt University Press.

Cohen B., Nestadt, G., Samuels, J., Romanoski, A., McHugh, P., & Rabins, P. (1994). Personality disorder in later life: A community study. *British Journal of Psychiatry* 165:493–9.

Cohen, C. (2000). Overcoming social amnesia: The role for a social perspective in psychiatric research and practice. *Psychiatric Services* 51: 72–8.

Coleman, R. (1999a). *Recovery? An alien concept*. Gloucester: Handsell.

Coleman, R. (1999b). Hearing voices and the politics of oppression. In C Newnes, G. Holmes, & C. Dunn (eds), *This is madness*. Ross on Wye: PCCS Books.

Coleman, R., & Smith, M. (1997). *Working with voices: From victim to victor*. Gloucester: Handsell.

Colombo, A., Bendelow, G., Fulford, K., & Williams, S. (2003). Evaluating the influence of implicit models of mental disorder on processes of shared decision making within community-based multidisciplinary teams. *Social Science & Medicine*, 56: 1557–70.

Copeland, M.E. (1997). *Wellness recovery action plan*. Brattleboro, VT: Peach Press.

Coppock, V., & Hopton, J. (2000). *Critical perspectives on mental health*. London: Routledge.

Corstens, D., Longden, E., & May, R. (2009). *Talking to voices.* http://intervoiceonline.org/2009/9/20/talking-to-voices-by-dirk-corstens-eleanor-longden-and-rufus-may

Coyle, D. (2009). *Recovery budgets in a mental health service.* University of Chester/Mersey Care NHS Trust. www.dhcarenetworks.org.uk/_library/Resources/Personalhealthbudgets/IRB_pilot_report_FINAL.pdf

Crowe, M., & Carlyle, D. (2003). Deconstructing risk assessment and management in mental health nursing *Journal of Advanced Nursing* 43(1): 19–26.

Cullberg, J. (2006). Integrated treatment and implications for off-medication periods. *Schizophrenia Bulletin* 32(2): 299.

Davies, T (2006) *Mental illness to recovery: We hold our own journey plans.* www.scottishrecovery.net/Submitted-thoughts-and-stories/Page-9.html

Deegan, P. (1988). Recovery: the lived experience of rehabilitation. *Psychosocial Rehabilitation Journal* 11:4 11–19.

Deegan, P. (1989). *Spirit breaking: When the helping professions hurt.* Presented at Phenomenal psychology and clinical practice, Duquesne University, Pittsburgh, PA. Text available via National Empowerment Center, Lawrence, MA.

Deegan, P. (1992). The independent living movement and people with psychiatric disabilities: Taking back control over our own lives. *Psychosocial Rehabilitation Journal* 15(3): 3–19.

Deegan, P. (1996) Recovery as a journey of the heart. *Psychiatric Rehabilitation Journal* 19, 91–97.

Deegan, P. (1997). Recovery and empowerment for people with psychiatric disabilities. *Social Work in Health Care* 25(3): 11–24.

Department of Health (1990). *The Care Programme Approach for people with a severe mental illness referred to specialist psychiatric services.* London: Department of Health.

Department of Health (2002). *Women's mental health: Into the mainstream.* London: Department of Health.

Department of Health (2004). *The Ten Essential Shared Capabilities: A framework for the whole of the mental health workforce.* London: Department of Health.

Department of Health (2005). *Delivering race equality in mental health care.* London: Department of Health.

Department of Health (2007). *Putting people first: A shared vision and commitment to the transformation of adult social care.* London: Department of Health.

Department of Health (2008). *Refocusing the Care Programme Approach: policy and positive practice guidance.* London: Department of Health.

Department of Health (2009). *New Horizons: A shared vision for mental health.* London: Department of Health. http://newhorizons.dh.gov.uk/Resources/reports/New-Horizons/index.aspx

Doel, M., & Marsh, P. (2003). *Task-centred social work.* Aldershot: Gower.

Dohrenwend, B.P. (2000). The role of adversity and stress in psychopathology: Some evidence and its implication for theory and research. *Journal of Health and Social Behavior* 41(1): 1–19.

Dohrenwend, B.S., Askenasy, A., Krasnoff, L., & Dohrenwend, B.P. (1978). Exemplification of a method of scaling life events. *Journal of Health and Social Behaviour* 19(2): 205–29.

Dominelli, L. (2002). *Anti-oppressive social work theory and practice.* Basingstoke: Palgrave Macmillan.

Douglas, M. (1992). *Risk and blame: Essays in cultural theory.* London: Routledge.

Drake, R., McHugo, G., Becker, D., Anthony, W., & Clark, R. (1996). The New Hampshire study of supported employment for people with severe mental illness. *Journal of Consulting and Clinical Psychology* 64(2): 391–9.

DuGay, P. , Evans, J., & Redman, P. (2000). *Identity.* London: Sage.

Duckworth, A., Steen, T., & Seligman, M. (2005). Positive psychology in clinical practice. *American Review of Clinical Psychology* 1: 629–51.

Dumont, J., & Jones, K. (2007). The crisis hostel. In P. Stastny & P. Lehmann (eds), *Alternatives beyond psychiatry.* Berlin: Peter Lehmann.

Duncombe, J., & Marsden, D. (1993). Love and intimacy: The gender division of emotion and 'emotion work'. *Sociology* 27(2): 221–41.

Elliot, A. (2007). *Concepts of the self* (2nd ed.). Cambridge: Polity.

Ellis, A. (2001). *Overcoming destructive beliefs, feelings, and behaviors: New directions for rational emotive behavior therapy.* New York: Prometheus Books.

Evans, J., & Fowler, R. (2008). *Family minded: Supporting children in families affected by mental illness.* Ilford: Barnardo's.

Fadden, G. (2006). Family interventions. In G Roberts, S. Davenport, F. Holloway, & T. Tattan (eds), *Enabling recovery.* London: Gaskell, pp. 158–69.

Falloon, I., & Fadden, G. (1993). *Integrated mental health care.* Cambridge: Cambridge University Press.

Falloon, I. R. H., McGill, C. W., Matthews, S. M., *et al.* (1996). Family treatment for schizophrenia: the design and research application of therapist training models. *Journal of Psychotherapy Practice and Research* 5: 45–56.

Fanon, F. (1967). *Black skins, white masks.* New York: Grove Press.

Fearon, P., Kirkbride, J., Dazzan, P., Morgan, C., Morgan, K., Lloyd, T., Hutchinson, G., Tarrant, J., Fung, W., Holloway, J., Mallett, R., Harrison, G., Leff, J., Jones, P., & Murray, R. (2006). Incidence of schizophrenia and other psychoses in ethnic minority groups: Results from the MRC AESOP Study. *Psychological Medicine* 26: 1–10.

Featherstone, B., Rivett, M., & Scourfield, J. (2007). *Working with men in health and social care.* London: Sage.

Felton, A., & Stacey, G. (2008). Positive risk taking: A framework for practice. In T. Stickley & T. Bassett (eds), *Learning about mental health practice.* Chichester: Wiley.

Fernando, S. (2010). *Mental health, race and culture* (3rd ed.). Basingstoke: Palgrave Macmilan.

Ferns, P. (2005). Finding a way forward: A black perspective on social approaches to mental health. In J Tew (ed.), *Social perspectives in mental health.* London: Jessica Kingsley.

Fish, F. (1966). The concept of schizophrenia. *British Journal of Medical Psychology* 39: 266–73.

Fisher, D. (1994). Vision of recovery. *Journal of the California Alliance for the Mentally Ill* 5(3): 1–2.

Fitzsimons, S., & Fuller, R. (2002). Empowerment and its implications for clinical practice in mental health. *Journal of Mental Health* 11(5): 481–99.

Fook, J. (2002). *Social work: Critical theory and practice.* London: Sage.

Foster, J. (2007). *Journeys through mental illness: Client experiences and understandings of mental distress.* Basingstoke: Palgrave Macmillan.

Foucault, M. (1967). *Madness and civilisation.* London: Tavistock.

Foucault, M. (1981). *The history of sexuality*, Vol.1. Harmondsworth: Penguin.

Foucault, M. (1982). The subject and power. In H. Dreyfuss & P. Rabinow (eds), *Michel Foucault: Beyond structuralism and hermeneutics.* Chicago: University of Chicago Press.

Fowler, D., Hodgekins, J., Howells, L., Millward, M., Ivins, A., Taylor, G., Hackmann, C., Hil, K., Bishop, N., & Macmillan, I. (2009). Can targeted early intervention improve functional recovery in psychosis? A historical control evaluation of the effectiveness of different models of early intervention service provision in Norfolk 1998–2007. *Early Intervention in Psychiatry* 3(4): 282–8.

Fraser, N., & Honneth, A. (2003). *Redistribution or recognition? A political-philosophical exchange*. London: Verso.

Frederick, J. (1991). *Positive thinking for mental health*. London: Black Mental Health Group.

Frenkel, E., Kugelmass, S., Nathan, M., & Ingraham, L. (1995). Locus of control and mental health in adolescence and adulthood. *Schizophrenia Bulletin* 21: 219–26.

Freud, A. (1968). *The ego and the mechanisms of defence* (revised ed). London: Hogarth Press.

Fryer, D. (1995). Labour market disadvantage, deprivation and mental health. *Psychologist* 8(6): 265–72.

Fryers, T., Meltzer, D., & Jenkins, R. (2001). *Mental health inequalities report 1: A systematic literature review*. Department of Public Health and Primary Care, U niversity of Cambridge.

Geekie, J. (2004). Listening to the voices we hear: Clients' understandings of psychotic experiences. In J. Read, L. Mosher, & R Bentnall (eds), *Models of madness*. Hove: Brunner-Routledge.

Germain, C., & Gitterman, A. (1996). The life model of social work practice (2nd ed.). New York: Columbia University Press.

Gilbert, P. (1992). *Depression: The evolution of powerlessness*. Hove: Lawrence Erlbaum.

Gilbert, P., & Allen, S. (1998). The role of defeat and entrapment (arrested flight) in depression: An exploration of an evolutionary view. *Psychological Medicine* 28: 585–98.

Gilbert, P., & Leahy, R. (2007). *The therapeutic relationship in cognitive behavioural therapies*. London: Routledge.

Glasby, J., & Littlechild, R. (2009). *Direct payments and personal budgets: Putting personalisation into practice*. Bristol: Policy Press.

Glasgow Anti-Stigma Partnership (2007). *Mosaics of Meaning: Summary report*. www.seemescotland.org.uk/images/pdfs

Glover, H. (2003). *Values and mental health recovery*. Paper presented to Conference on the Role of Values in Mental Health. London, March. www.connects.org.uk/conferences/pkgs/conference_centre/conference_papers.asp

Glynn, S., Cohen, A., Dixon, L., & Niv, N. (2006). The potential impact of the recovery movement on family interventions for schizophrenia. *Schizophrenia Bulletin* 32(3): 451–63.

Goffman, E. (1963). *Stigma: Notes on the management of a spoiled identity*. Englewood Cliffs, NJ: Prentice Hall.

Golan, N. (1986). Crisis theory. In F. Turner (ed.), *Social work treatment: Interlocking theoretical approaches*. New York: Free Press.

Goldapple, K., Segal, Z., Garson, C., Lau, M., Bieling, P., Kennedy, S., & Mayberg, H. (2004). Modulation of cortical-limbic pathways in major depression: Treatment-specific effects of cognitive behaviour therapy. *Archives of General Psychiatry* 61: 34–41.

Goldstein, M. (1985). Family factors that antedate the onset of schizophrenia and related disorders. *Acta Psychiatrica Scandinavica* 71(suppl. 319): 7–18.

Goleman, D. (1995). *Emotional intelligence*. New York: Bantam.

Gopfort, M., Webster, J., & Seeman, M. (eds) (2004). *Parental psychiatric disorder: Distressed parents and their families*. Cambridge: Cambridge University Press.

Gorell-Barnes, G. (1998). *Family therapy in changing times*. Basingstoke: Macmillan.

Green, L., Oades, L., & Grant, A. (2006). Cognitive-behavioural, solution-focused life coaching: Enhancing goal striving, well-being and hope. *Journal of Positive Psychology* 1(3): 142–9.

Hall, S. (2000). Who needs identity? In P. du Gay, J. Evans, & P. Redman (eds), *Identify*. London: Sage.

Halpern, D., & Nazroo, J. (2000). The ethnic density effect. *International Journal of Social Psychiatry* 46: 34–6.

Hammersley, P., & McLaughlin, T. (2006). *The Campaign for Abolition of the Schizophrenia Label*. casl@asylumonline.net

Hamner, M., Frueh, B, Ulmer, H., Huber, M., Twomey, T., Tyson, C., & Arana, G. (2000). Psychotic features in chronic posttraumatic stress disorder and schizophrenia: Comparative severity. *Journal of Nervous and Mental Disease* 188: 217–19.

Harding, C., Brooks, G., Takamaru, A., Strauss, J., & Breier, A. (1987). The Vermont longitudinal study of persons with severe mental illness. *American Journal of Psychiatry* 144(6): 718–35.

Harrison, G., Gunnell, D., Glazebrook, C., Page, K., & Kwiecinski, R. (2001). Association between schizophrenia and social inequality at birth: Case control study. *British Journal of Psychiatry* 179: 346–50.

Hartman, A. (1995). Diagramatic assessment of family relationships. *Families in Society* 76: 111–22.

Healy, K. (2005). *Social work theories in context*. Basingstoke: Palgrave Macmillan.

Helliwell, C., & Hindess, B. (1999). Power. In S. Taylor (ed.), *Sociology: Issues and debates*. Basingstoke: Palgrave Macmillan.

Herman, J. (1997). *Trauma and recovery: The aftermath of violence from domestic abuse to political terror*. New York: Basic Books.

Herman, J., & Schatzow, E. (1987). Recovery and verification of childhood sexual trauma. *Psychoanalytic Psychology* 4: 1–14.

Hermans, H. (2003). The construction and reconstruction of the dialogical self. *Journal of Constructivist Psychology* 162: 89–130.

Hickling, F., & Rodgers-Johnson, P. (1995). The incidence of first-contact schizophrenia in Jamaica. *British Journal of Psychiatry* 175: 283–5.

Hiday, V.A. (2006). Putting community risk in perspective: A look at correlations, causes and controls. *International Journal of Law and Psychiatry* 29: 316–31.

Higgins, E. (1987). Self discrepancy: A theory relating self and affect. *Psychological Review* 94(3): 319–40.

Hilgartner, S. (1992). The social construction of risk objects: Or how to pry open networks of risk. In J. Short & L. Clarke (eds), *Organisations, uncertainties and risk*. Boulder, CO: Westview Press, pp. 39–53.

Hill, P. (2008). *Living out of the book*. Brentwood: Chipmunka.

Hodgins, S., & Müller-Isberner, R. (2004). Preventing crime by people with schizophrenic disorders: The role of psychiatric services. *British Journal of Psychiatry* 185: 245–50.

Holley, T. (2007). *A service user's perspective – the narrative edge*. Presentation delivered at Developing Excellence in Research Education and Practice Conference, North East Wales Institute of Higher Education, 11–13 June.

Hollin, C. (1997). *Criminal behaviour: A psychosocial approach to explanation and prevention*. Hove: Psychology Press.

Holloway, F. (1996). Community psychiatric care: from libertarianism to coercion: 'Moral panic' and mental health policy in Britain. *Health Care Analysis* 4: 235–43.

Holloway, J. (with E. Craig) (2009). Learning from voices. In J. Reynolds, R. Muston, T. Heller, J. Leach, M. McCormick, J. Wallcraft, & M. Walsh (eds), *Mental health still matters*. Basingstoke: Palgrave Macmillan.

Hollway, W. (2009). Relationality: The intersubjective foundations of identity. In M. Wetherell, & C. Mohanty (eds), *Handbook of identities*. London: Sage, pp. 216–33.

Holowka, D. et al., (2003). Childhood abuse and dissociative symptoms in adult schizophrenia. *Schizophrenia Research* 60: 87–90.

Hornstein, G. (2009). *Agnes's jacket: A psychologist's search for the meanings of madness*. New York: Rodale.

Howell, E. (2005). *The dissociative mind*. London: Analytic Press.

Hoyer, G (2008). Involuntary hospitalisation in contemporary mental health care: Some (still) unanswered questions. *Journal of Mental Health* 17: 281–92.

Hutton, P. (2008). *A heuristic exploration of 'depression' and 'recovery' conducted through the medium of autoethnography*. MA Dissertation. University of East London.

Ingleby, D. (1981). *Critical psychiatry*. Harmondsworth: Penguin.

Janssen, I., Hanssen, M., Bak, M., Bijl, R., De Graaf, R., Vollebergh, W., Mckenzie, K., & Van Os, J. (2003). Discrimination and delusional ideation. *British Journal of Psychiatry* 182: 71–6.

Jaspers, K. (1913). *Allgemeine Psychopathologie: Ein Leitfaden für Studierende, Ärzte und Psychologen*, Berlin: Springer. [*General Psychopathology*, trans. J. Hoenig & M.W. Hamilton, Chicago: University of Chicago Press, 1963.]

Johnson, S., & Needle, J. (2008). Introduction and concepts. In S Johnson, J. Needle, J. Bindman, & G. Thornicroft (eds), *Crisis resolution and home treatment in mental health*. Cambridge: Cambridge University Press.

Johnstone, L. (1999) Do families cause 'schizophrenia'? Revisiting a taboo subject. In C Newnes, G. Holmes, & C. Dunn (eds), *This is madness*. Ross on Wye: PCCS Books.

Jorm, A., Korten, A., Rodgers, B., Jacomber, P., & Christiansen, H. (2002). Sexual orientation and mental health: Results from a community survey of young and middle-aged adults. *British Journal of Psychiatry* 180: 423–7.

Kahler, T. (1974). The miniscript. *Transactional Analysis Journal* 4(1): 26–42.

Kanel, K. (2003). *A guide to crisis intervention*. Pacific Grove, CA: Brooks/Cole.

Keating, F. (2002). *Breaking the circles of fear*. London: Sainsbury Centre for Mental Health.

Keijsers, G., Schaap, C., & Hoogduin, C. (2000). The impact of interpersonal patient and therapist behaviour on outcome in cognitive behaviour therapy: A review of empirical studies. *Behaviour Modification* 24(2): 264–97.

Kemshall, H. (2002). *Risk, social policy and welfare*. Buckingham: Open University Press.

Keown, P., Holloway, F., & Kuipers, E. (2002). The prevalence of personality disorders, psychotic disorders and affective disorders amongst the patients seen by a community mental health team in London. *Social Psychiatry and Psychiatric Epidemiology* 32(5): 225–9.

Kilcommons, A., & Morrison, A. (2005). Relationships between trauma and psychosis: An exploration of cognitive and dissociative factors. *Acta Psychiatrica Scandanavica* 112(5): 351–9.

Kilmartin, C. (2005). Depression in men: Communication, diagnosis and therapy. *Journal of Men's Health and Gender* 2(1): 95–9.

Kilshaw, S. (with D. Ndegwa & J. Curran) (2002). *Between worlds: Interpreting conflict between black patients and clinicians*. London: Lambeth, Southwark and Lewisham Health Action Zone.

Kinderman, P. (2005). A psychological model of mental disorder. *Harvard Review of Psychiatry* 13: 206–17.

Kinderman, P., Sellwood, W., & Tai, S. (2008). Policy implications of a psychological model of mental disorder. *Journal of Mental Health* 17(1): 93–103.

King, M., McKeown, E., Warner, J., Ramsay, A., Johnson, K., Cort, C., Wright, L., Blizard, R., & Davidson, O. (2003). Mental health and quality of life of gay men and lesbians in England and Wales. *British Journal of Psychiatry* 183: 552–8.

Kiseley, S., Xiao, J., & Preston, N. (2004). Impact of compulsory community treatment on admission rates. *British Journal of Psychiatry* 184(5): 432–8.

Kobasa, S.C. (1979). Stressful life events, personality and health: An inquiry into hardiness. *Journal of Personality and Social Psychology* 37: 1–11.

Kolodziej, M., & Johnson B. (1996). Interpersonal contact and acceptance of persons with psychiatric disorders: A research synthesis. *Journal of Consulting Clinical Psychology* 64: 387–96.

Kuipers, L., Bebbington, P., Dunn, G., Fowler, D. Freeman, D., Watson, P. Hardy, A., & Garety, P. (2006). Influence of carer expressed emotion and affect on relapse in non-affective psychosis. *British Journal of Psychiatry* 188: 173–9.

Kuipers, L., Leff, J., & Lam, D. (1992). *Family work for schizophrenia.* London: Gaskell.

Langan, J., & Lindow, V. (2004). *Living with risk: Mental health service user involvement in risk assessment and management.* Bristol: Policy Press.

Larkin, W., & Morrison, A. (2006). *Trauma and psychosis: New directions for theory and therapy.* Hove: Routledge.

Laurance, J. (2003). *Pure madness: How fear drives the mental health system.* London: Routledge.

Lawrence, M. (1984) *The anorexic experience.* London: Women's Press.

Layard, R. (2006) *Happiness: Lessons from a new science.* London: Penguin.

Leete, E. (1989) How I perceive and manage my illness. *Schizophrenia Bulletin* 15: 197–200.

Lefevre, S. (1996). *Killing me softly. Self-harm: Survival not suicide.* Gloucester: Handsell.

Lexmond, J., & Reeves, R. (2009). *Building character.* London: Demos.

Lidz, T. (1975). *The origin and treatment of schizophrenic disorders.* London: Hutchinson.

Link, B., & Phelan, J. (2001). Conceptualising stigma. *Annual Review of Sociology* 27: 363–5.

Lipschitz, D. (1999). Perceived abuse and neglect as risk factors for suicidal behaviour in adolescent inpatients. *Journal of Nervous and Mental Disease* 187: 32–9.

Lipsky, S. (1987). *Internalised racism.* Seattle: Rational Island Publishers.

Lukes, S. (2005). *Power: A radical view* (2nd ed.). Basingstoke: Palgrave Macmillan.

Lysaker, P., Roe, D., & Yanos, P. (2009). The role of insight in the process of recovery from schizophrenia: A review of three views. *Psychosis* 1(2): 113–21.

MacKeith, J., & Burns, S. (2010). *The Recovery Star: User Guide* (2nd ed.) and *The Recovery Star: Organisation Guide* (2nd ed.). London Mental Health Providers Forum.

Maercker, A., Michael, T., Fehm, L., Becker, E.S., & Margraf, J. (2004). Age of traumatisation as a predictor of post-traumatic stress disorder or major depression in young women. *British Journal of Psychiatry* 184: 482–7.

Mancini, A., & Bonamo, G. (2006). Resilience in the face of potential trauma: Clinical practices and illustrations. *Journal of Clinical Psychology: In Session* 62(8): 971–85.

Mancini, M. (2007). The role of self-efficacy in recovery from serious psychiatric disabilities. *Qualitative Social Work* 6(1): 49–74.

Marsh, P., & Crow, G. (1998). *Family group conferences in child welfare.* Oxford: Blackwell.

Masterson, S., & Owen, S. (2006). Mental health service users' social and individual empowerment. *Journal of Mental Health* 15(1): 19–34.

McAuley, C., & Young, C. (2006). The mental health needs of looked-after children: Challenges for CAMHS provision. *Journal of Social Work Practice* 20: 91–103.

McClean, C., Campbell, C., & Cornfish, F. (2002). African-Caribbean interactions with mental health services in the UK: Experiences and expectations of exclusions as (re)productive of health inequalities. *Social Science and Medicine* 56(3): 657–69.

McCrone, P., Dhanasiri, S., & Knapp, M. (2006). Modelling the impact of early intervention services. *Schizophrenia Research* 86(suppl.): S61–2.

McFarlane, L. (1998). *Diagnosis: homophobic – the experience of lesbians, gay men and bisexuals in mental health services.* London: PACE.

McGovern, D., & Cope, R. (1987). First psychiatric admission rates of first and second generation Afro-Caribbeans. *Social Psychiatry* 122: 139–40.

Mead, S., & MacNeil C. (2006). Peer support: What makes it unique? *International Journal of Psychosocial Rehabilitation* 10(2): 29–37.

Mental Health Foundation (2002). *Out at work: A survey of the experiences of people with mental health problems within the workplace.* London: Mental Health Foundation.

Mezzina, R., Davidson, L., Borg, M., Marin, I., Topor, A., & Sells, D. (2006). The social nature of recovery: Discussion and implications for practice. *American Journal of Psychiatric Rehabilitation* 9: 63–80.

Monahan, J. (1993). Dangerousness: An American perspective. In J. Gunn & P. Taylor (eds), *Forensic psychiatry.* London: Butterworth-Heinemann.

Moncrieff, J. (2008). *The myth of the chemical cure: A critique of psychiatric drug treatment.* Basingstoke: Palgrave Macmillan.

Moon, L. (1996). Working with single people. In D. Davies & C. Neal (eds), *Pink therapy.* Buckingham: Open University Press.

Moran, P., & Eckenrode, J. (1992). Protective personality characteristics among adolescent victims of maltreatment. &*Child Abuse and Neglect* 16(5): 743–54.

Mosher, L. (2004). Non-hospital intervention with first episode psychosis. In J. Read, L. Mosher, & R. Bentnall (eds), *Models of madness.* Hove: Brunner Routledge.

Mullen, R., Gibbs, A., & Dawson J. (2006). Family perspective on community treatment orders: A New Zealand study. *International Journal of Social Psychiatry* 52(5): 469–78.

Mulligan, K. (2001). Psychiatrist turns illness into empowerment tool. *Psychiatric News* 36(11): 17. www.pn.psychiatryonline.org/cgi/full/36/11/17

Munro, E., & Rumgay, J. (2000). Role of risk assessment in reducing homicides by people with mental illness. *British Journal of Psychiatry* 176: 116–20.

Needham, C., & Carr, S. (2009). *Co-production: An emerging evidence base for adult social care transformation.* SCIE Research Briefing 31. London: Social Care Institute for Excellence.

Nelson, G., Lord, J., & Ochocka, J. (2001a). Empowerment and mental health in community: Narratives of psychiatric consumer/survivors. *Journal of Community and Applied Social Psychology* 11: 125–42.

Nelson, G., Lord, J., & Ochocka, J. (2001b). *Shifting the paradigm in community mental health: Towards empowerment and community.* Toronto: Toronto University Press.

Office of National Statistics (2003). *Better or worse: A longitudinal study of the mental health of adults in Britain.* London: Office of National Statistics.

O'Hagan, M. (2009). Two accounts of mental distress. In J. Reynolds, R. Muston, T. Heller, J. Leach, M. McCormick, J. Wallcraft, & M. Walsh (eds), *Mental health still matters*. Basingstoke: Palgrave Macmillan, pp. 198–204.

Oliver, M. (1996). *Understanding disability: From theory to practice*. Basingstoke. Macmillan.

Otis, M., & Skinner, W. (1996). The prevalence of victimisation and its effect on mental well-being among lesbian and gay people. *Journal of Homosexuality* 30(3): 93–121.

Pembroke, L. (2009). Harm-minimisation: Limiting the damage of self-injury. In J. Reynolds, R. Muston, T. Heller, J. Leach, M. McCormick, J. Wallcraft, & M. Walsh (eds), *Mental health still matters*. Basingstoke: Palgrave Macmillan, pp. 231–3.

Pennings, M., & Romme, M. (2000). Hearing voices in patient and non-patients. In M. Romme (ed.), *Understanding voices*. Gloucester: Handsell.

Perry, B., Pollard, R., Blakely, T., Baker, W., & Vigilante, D. (1995). Childhood trauma, the neurobiology of adaptation, and 'use-dependent' development of the brain: How states become traits. *Infant Mental Health Journal* 16: 271–91.

Petch, E. (2001). Risk management in UK mental health services – an overvalued idea? *Psychiatric Bulletin* 25: 203–5.

Pettie, D., & Triolo, A. (1999). Illness as evolution: The search for identity and meaning in the recovery process. *Psychiatric Rehabilitation Journal* 22(3): 255–62.

Pinkerton, J., & Dolan, P. (2007). Family support, social capital, resilience and adolescent coping. *Child and Family Social Work* 12(3): 219–28.

Plumb, A. (1999). New mental health legislation. A lifesaver? Changing paradigm and practice. *Social Work Education* 18(4): 459–78.

Plumb, S. (2005). The social/trauma model. In J. Tew (ed.), *Social perspectives in mental health*. London: Jessica Kingsley.

Polak, P. (1971). Social systems intervention. *Archives of General Psychiatry* 25: 110–17.

Porter, R. (1987). *A social history of madness: Stories of the insane*. London: Weidenfield, & Nicolson.

Power, P., MCGuire, P., Iacoponi, E., Garety, P., Morris, E., Valmaggia, L., Grafton, D., & Craig, T. (2007). Early intervention in the real world: Lambeth Early Onset (LEO) and Outreach Support in South London (OASIS) service. *Early Intervention in Psychiatry* 1(1): 97–103.

Prior, P. (1999). *Gender and mental health*. Basingstoke: Macmillan.

Prouty, G., Van Werde, D., & Portner, M. (2002). *Pre-therapy: Reaching contact-impaired adults*. Ross on Wye: PCCS Books.

Puttnam, R. (1996). The strange disappearance of civic America. *American Prospect* 7(24): 34–48.

Ralph, R., Risman, J., Kidder, K., & Recovery Advisory Group (1999). *The Recovery Advisory Group recovery model.* Washington, DC: National Conference on Mental Health Statistics, June.

Ramon, S. (2005). Approaches to risk in mental health discourse. In J. Tew (ed.), *Social perspectives in mental health.* London: Jessica Kingsley.

Read, J. (2004) Poverty, ethnicity and gender. In J. Read, L. Mosher, & R. Bentnall (eds), *Models of madness.* Hove: Brunner Routledge.

Read, J., & Baker, S. (1996) *Not just sticks and stones: A survey of the stigma, taboos and discrimination experienced by people with mental health problems.* London: MIND.

Read, J., Haslam, N., Sayce, L., & Davies, E. (2006). Prejudice and schizophrenia: A review of the 'mental illness is an illness like any other' approach. *Acta Psychiatrica Scandanavica* 114: 303–18.

Read, J., Van Os, J., Morrison, A., & Ross, C. (2005). Childhood trauma, psychosis and schizophrenia: A literature review with theoretical and clinical implications. *Acta Psychiatrica Scandanavica* 112(5): 330–50.

Reivich, K., & Shatté, A. (2002). *The resilience factor.* New York: Broadway Books.

Repper, J., & Perkins, R. (2003). *Social inclusion and recovery.* London: Baillière Tindall.

Repper, J., Grant, G., Nolan, M., & Enderby, P. (2008). Carers' experiences of mental health services and views about assessments. In T. Stickley & T. Basset (eds), *Learning about mental health practice.* Chichester: Wiley.

Richardson, G. (2008). Coercion and human rights: A European perspective. *Journal of Mental Health* 17: 245–54.

Ridge, D., & Ziebland, S. (2006). 'The old me could not have done that': How people give meaning to recovery following depression. *Qualitative Health Research* 16(8): 1038–53.

Roberts, A. (ed.) (2000). *Crisis intervention handbook.* Oxford: Oxford University Press.

Roe, D., & Davidson, L. (2005). Self and narrative in schizophrenia: Time to author a new story. *Medical Humanities* 31: 89–94.

Roffman, J., Marci, C., Glick, D., Dougherty, D., & Rauch, S. (2005). Neuroimaging and the functional neuroanatomy of psychotherapy. *Psychological Medicine* 35(1): 1385–98.

Rogers, A., & Pilgrim, D. (2003). *Mental health and inequality.* Basingstoke: Palgrave Macmillan.

Romme, M., & and Escher, S. (1993). *Accepting voices.* London: MIND.

Romme, M., & Escher, S. (2000). Empowering people who hear voices. In M. Romme (ed.), *Understanding voices*. Gloucester: Handsell.

Rutter, M. (1990). Psychosocial resilience and protective mechanisms. In J. Rolf, A. Masten, D. Cicchetti, K. Neuchterlein, & S. Weintraub (eds), *Risk and protective factors in the development of psychopathology*. New York: Cambridge University Press.

Ryan, R., & Deci, E. (2001). On happiness and human potential: A review of research on hedonic and eudaimonic well-being. *Annual Review of Psychology* 52: 141–66.

Sainsbury Centre for Mental Health (2001). *Crisis resolution*. London: Sainsbury Centre for Mental Health.

Saleebey, D. (2006). *The strengths perspective in social work practice* (4th ed). New York: Allyn & Bacon.

Salovey, P., Bedell, B., Detweiler, J., & Mayer, J. (1999). Coping intelligently: Emotional intelligence and the coping process. In C. Snyder (ed.), *Coping: The psychology of what works*. New York: Oxford University Press, pp. 141–64.

Sanderson, H. (2000). *Person-centred planning: Key features and approaches*. York: Joseph Rowntree Foundation.

Sayce, L. (2000). *From psychiatric patient to citizen: Overcoming discrimination and social exclusion*. Basingstoke: Palgrave Macmillan.

Schnyder, U. (1997). Crisis intervention in psychiatric outpatients. *International Medical Journal* 4(1): 11–17.

Schon, U.-K., Denhov, A., & Topor, A. (2009). Social relationships as a decisive factor in recovering from serious mental illness. *International Journal of Social Psychiatry* 55(4): 336–47.

Scott, J., Chant, D., Andrews, G., Martin, G., & McGrath, J. (2007). Association between trauma exposure and delusional experiences in a large community-based sample. *British Journal of Psychiatry* 190: 339–43.

Scottish Recovery Network (2006) *Journeys of Recovery*. www.scottishrecovery.net/Narrative-Research-Project/narrative-research-project.html

Scottish Recovery Network (2008). *Finding strength from within*. www.scottishrecovery.net/view-document/68

Scottish Recovery Network (2009). *Carers and supporting recovery*. www.scottishrecovery.net/view-document/236

Seligman, M. (1974). Depression and learned helplessness. In R. Friedman & M. Katz (eds), *The psychology of depression: Contemporary theory and research*. Washington, DC: Winston.

Seligman, M.E.P. (1991). *Learned optimism*. New York: Pocket Books.

Selten, J.-P., & Cantor-Graae, E. (2007). Hypothesis: Social defeat as a risk factor for schizophrenia. *British Journal of Psychiatry* 191(suppl. 51): S9–12.

Shaw, J., Hunt, I., Flynn, S., Meehan, M., Robinson, J., Bickley, H., Parsons, R., McCann, K., Burns, J., Amos, T., Kapur, N., & Appleby, L. (2006). Rates of mental disorder in people convicted of homicide. National clinical survey. *British Journal of Psychiatry* 188: 143–7.

Shergill, S., & Szmukler,G. (1998). How predictable is violence and suicide in community psychiatric practice? *Journal of Mental Health* 7(4): 393–401.

Shevlin, M., Houston, J., Dorahy, M., & Adamson, G. (2008). Cumulative traumas and psychosis: An analysis of the National Comorbidity Survey and the British Psychiatric Morbidity Survey. *Schizophrenia Bulletin* 34(1):193–99.

Shonkoff, J., & Phillips, D. (2000). *From neurons to neighbourhoods: The science of early development.* Washington, DC: National Academy Press.

Sibitz, I., Unger, A., Woppman, A., Zidek, T., & Amering, M. (2009). Stigma resistance in patients with schizophrenia. *Schizophrenia Bulletin* doi:10.1093/schbul/sbp048.

Simpson, A., McKenna, B., Moskowitz, A., Skipworth, J., & Barry-Walsh, J. (2004). Homicide and mental illness in New Zealand, 1970–2000. *British Journal of Psychiatry* 185: 394–8.

Singh, S., Greenwood, N., White, S., & Churchill, R. (2007). Ethnicity and the Mental Health Act 1983. *British Journal of Psychiatry* 191: 99–105.

Slade, M. (2009). *Personal recovery and mental illness: A guide for mental health professionals.* Cambridge: Cambridge University Press.

Smale, G., Tuson, G., Biehal, N., & Marsh, P. (1998). *Empowerment, assessment, care management and the skilled worker* (2nd ed.). London: National Institute for Social Work.

Smith, J., & Shiers, D. (2009). Catching them young. *Mental Health Today* 10(5): 32–3.

Social Care Institute for Excellence, Royal College of Psychiatrists and Care Services Improvement Partnership (2007). *Position Paper 8: A common purpose: Recovery in future mental health services.* London: Social Care Institute for Excellence.

Social Exclusion Unit (2004). *Mental health and social exclusion.* London: Office of the Deputy Prime Minister.

Somers, M. (1994). The narrative constitution of identity: A relational and network approach. *Theory and Society* 23: 635–49.

Spaniol, L., & Gagne, C. (1997). Acceptance: Some reflections. *Psychiatric Rehabilitation Journal* 20(3): 75–8.

Stastny, P., & Lehmann, P. (eds) (2007). *Alternatives beyond psychiatry.* Berlin: Peter Lehmann.

Stevenson, F., & Zimmerman, M.A. (2005). Adolescent resilience: A framework for understanding healthy development in the face of risk. *Annual Review of Public Health* 26: 399–419.

Stickley, T., & Felton, A. (2006). Promoting recovery through therapeutic risk-taking. *Mental Health Practice* 9(8): 26–30.

Surrey, J. (1985). *Self-in-relation: A theory of women's development.* Wellesley, MA: Stone Center Working Paper Series.

Swanson, J., Swartz, M., Elbogen, E., Van Dorn, R., Wagner, H., Moser, L., Wilder, C., & Gilbert, A. (2008). Psychiatric advance directives and reduction of coercive crisis interventions. *Journal of Mental Health* 17(3): 255–67.

Swartz, M., Wagner, H., Swanson, J., & Elbogen, E. (2004). Consumers' perceptions of the fairness and effectiveness of mandated community treatment and related pressures. *Psychiatric Services* 55(7): 780–5.

Szasz, T. (1961). *The myth of mental illness: Foundations of a theory of personal conduct.* New York: Harper & Row.

Szmukler, G., & Appelbaum, P. (2008). Treatment pressures, leverage and compulsion in mental health care. *Journal of Mental Health* 17: 233–44.

Taylor, P., & Gunn, J. (1999). Homicides by people with mental illness: Myth and reality. *British Journal of Psychiatry* 174: 9–14.

Tew, J. (1999). Voices from the margins: Inserting the social in mental health discourse. *Social Work Education* 18(4): 433–49.

Tew, J. (2002). *Social theory, power and practice.* Basingstoke: Palgrave Macmillan.

Tew, J. (ed.) (2005a). *Social perspectives in mental health.* London: Jessica Kingsley.

Tew, J. (2005b). Power relations, social order and mental distress. In J. Tew (ed.), *Social perspectives and mental health.* London: Jessica Kingsley.

Tew, J., Gould, N., Abankwa, D., Barnes, H., Beresford, P., Carr, S., Copperman, J., Ramon, S., Rose, D., Sweeney, A., & Woodward, L. (2006). *Values and methodologies for social research in mental health.* London: Social Perspectives Network/Social Care Institute for Excellence.

Thompson, N. (2006). *Anti-discriminatory practice.* Basingstoke: Palgrave Macmillan.

Tienari, P., Wynne, L.C., Sorri, A., Lahti, I., Laksy, K., Moring, J., Naarala, M., Nieminen, P., & Wahlberg, K.-E. (2004). Genotype–

environment interaction in schizophrenia-spectrum disorder: Long-term follow-up study of Finnish adoptees. *British Journal of Psychiatry* 184: 216–22.

Thornicroft, G. (2006). *Actions speak louder: Tackling discrimination against people with mental illness.* London: Mental Health Foundation.

Topor, A., Svensson, J., Bjerke, C., Kuftas, E., & Borg, M. (n.d.). *Turning points on the road to recovery from serious psychiatric illness.* FoU-enheten/psykiatri. VSPS.

Trivedi, P. (2008). Respecting diversity. In T. Stickley & T. Bassett (eds), *Learning about mental health practice.* Chichester: Wiley.

Tsang, H., Lam, P., Ng, B., & Leung, O. (2000). Predictors of employment outcome for people with psychiatric disabilities: A review of the literature since the mid-80s. *Journal of Rehabilitation* 66(2): 19–31.

Tyrer, P. (2007). Personality diathesis: A superior explanation than disorder. *Psychological Medicine* 37: 1521–5.

Van der Kolk, B,, Perry, C., & Herman, J. (1991). Childhood origins of self-destructive behaviour. *American Journal of Psychiatry* 148(12): 1665–71.

Van Os, J., Hanssen, M., Bijl, R., & Ravelli, A. (2000). Strauss (1969) revisited: A psychosis continuum in the general population? *Schizophrenia Research* 45: 11–20.

Wallcraft, J., & Michaelson, J. (2001). Developing a survivor discourse to replace the 'psychopathology' of breakdown and crisis. In C. Newnes, G. Holmes, & C. Dunn (eds), *This is madness too.* Ross on Wye: PCCS Books.

Walsh, M. (2009). (Mis)representing mental distress. In J. Reynolds, R. Muston, T. Heller, J. Leach, M. McCormick, J. Wallcraft, & M. Walsh (eds), *Mental health still matters.* Basingstoke: Palgrave Macmillan, pp. 135–40.

Warner, J. (2007). Structural stigma, institutional trust and the risk agenda in mental health policy. In T. Maltby & P. Kennett (eds), *Social Policy Review 19: Analysis and debate in social policy.* Bristol: Policy Press.

Warner, R. (1994). *Recovery from schizophrenia: Psychiatry and political economy.* New York: Routledge.

Warner, S. (2000). *Understanding child sexual abuse: Making the tactics visible.* Gloucester: Handsell.

Warren, K. (2003). *Exploring the concept of recovery from the perspective of people with mental health problems.* Norwich: UEA Social Work Monographs.

Westwood, S. (2002). *Power and the social.* London: Routledge.

White, M., & Epston, D. (1990). *Narrative means to therapeutic ends.* New York: W.W. Norton.

Wilkinson, J. (1998). Danger on the streets: Mental illness, community care and ingratitude. In A. Symonds & A. Kelly (eds), *The social construction of community care*. Basingstoke: Macmillan.

Wilkinson R.G. (2005). *The impact of inequality: How to make sick societies healthier*. London: Routledge.

Williams, A. (2009). The recovery of hope. In J. Reynolds, R. Muston, T. Heller, J. Leach, M. McCormick, J. Wallcraft, & M. Walsh (eds), *Mental health still matters*. Basingstoke: Palgrave Macmillan, pp. 218–20.

Williams, F. (2005). A good enough life: Developing a political 'ethic of care'. *Soundings* 30: 17–32.

Woodbridge K., & Fulford, K. (2004). *Whose values? A workbook for values-based practice in mental health care*. London: Sainsbury Centre for Mental Health.

World Health Organisation (2001). *Strengthening mental health promotion*. Factsheet 220. Geneva: World Health Organisation.

Wright, T. (2008). Using family group conference in mental health. *Nursing Times* 104(4): 34–5.

Young, S., & Ensing, D. (1999). Exploring recovery from the perspective of people with psychiatric disabilities. *Psychiatric Rehabilitation Journal* 222: 219–31.

Zinkler, M., & Priebe, S. (2002). Detention of the mentally ill in Europe: A review. *Acta Psychiatrica Scandanavica* 106: 3–8.

Zubin, J., & Spring R. (1977). Vulnerability: A new view of schizophrenia. *Journal of Abnormal Psychology* 86(2): 103–24.

Index